HERESY

ALSO BY MICHAEL COREN

Why Catholics Are Right (2011)

As I See It (2009)

J.R.R. Tolkien: The Man Who Created the Lord of the Rings (2001)

Setting It Right (1996)

The Man Who Created Narnia: The Story of C.S. Lewis (1994)

The Life of Sir Arthur Conan Doyle (1993)

The Invisible Man: The Life and Liberties of H.G. Wells (1993)

Aesthete (1993)

Gilbert: The Man Who Was G.K. Chesterton (1990)

The Outsiders (1985)

Theatre Royal: 100 Years of Stratford East (1985)

MICHAEL COREN
HERESY
TEN LIES THEY SPREAD ABOUT
CHRISTIANITY

SIGNAL

McCLELLAND
& STEWART

Signal is an imprint of McClelland & Stewart,
a division of Random House of Canada Limited.

Cloth edition published 2012
Paperback edition published 2013

Library and Archives Canada Cataloguing in Publication

Coren, Michael
Heresy : ten lies they spread about Christianity / Michael Coren.

Includes index.
ISBN 978-0-7710-2317-0

1. Christian heresies. 2. Theology, Doctrinal. 3. Apologetics. I. Title.

BT1315.3.C67 2013   273   C2012-904102-5

Typeset in Dante by M&S, Toronto
Printed and bound in Canada

McClelland & Stewart,
a division of Random House of Canada Limited
One Toronto Street
Toronto, Ontario
M5C 2V6
www.mcclelland.com

1   2   3   4   5   17   16   15   14   13

To Walter Hooper

CONTENTS

INTRODUCTION

IN THE SUMMER OF 2011, a horrendous mass murder occurred in Norway, with more than ninety people, most of them teenagers and even children, being slaughtered in a co-ordinated bomb and gun attack. Various Islamic groups initially claimed responsibility, and had been promising an attack on Norway for some time because of that country's commitment to the Afghanistan war, Oslo's prosecution of a specific Islamic war criminal, and Norway's refusal to ban the publication of a cartoon of Mohammad that many Muslims found offensive. The nature and implementation of the attack – first a diversionary explosion to attract security and emergency services, followed by a targeted gun slaughter – resembled the work of Islamic terror groups, who had perfected the approach in the Middle East and other parts of Europe. In the end, the killer, Anders Behring Breivik, was revealed to be a native blond, blue-eyed Norwegian, a strange and disturbed loner, whose motivation was partly political, and whose ideology seemed in some confused, confusing way to be based on an objection to Islam, multiculturalism, and Marxism. Yet within hours of Breivik's attack, there were countless accusations in newspapers and on radio and television that the gunman was a Christian fundamentalist, motivated by his evangelical Christian religion to hate progress, change, and, in particular, Muslims. Why, therefore, he should attack a group of young people who were themselves mostly Christians was not fully explored, especially when there were myriad Islamic targets in Norway. But the sudden, new, self-evident "fact" that he was a "Christian fundamental-ist" was repeated over and over again in media reports, until it was considered virtually treasonous to question the statement.

The reason he was now a Christian bogeyman was that he allegedly regarded himself as a Christian, and that he had posted some comments on a Christian fundamentalist blog. Flimsy evidence at best, but it was sufficient to set off anti-Christian alarm bells the world over. What was not really explained, or certainly understood or even taken into account, however, was that Breivik was an active Freemason, which was pretty obvious to anybody paying attention in that the standard photograph of him published by the media showed him posing in his Masonic regalia and apron. A journalist worth the name, or even an onlooker with any sense, would have realized that Christian fundamentalism regards Freemasonry as an anti-Christian cult, one that is more in league with the anti-Christ than Christ. Fundamentalist churches forbid Masons from being members of their congregations, as do most mainstream evangelical denominations. Roman Catholicism also condemns Freemasonry, and Catholic and evangelical publishers offer a series of books explaining why no follower of Christ can be a Mason. All of this, it seemed, was too esoteric and complex for the Christian-bashers who suddenly smelled relativism and blood. Or, perhaps, bloody relativism.

It also quickly emerged that Breivik was supportive of the gay community, which again would make him an impossible fundamentalist. Nor did he have any known affiliation to any church, which is crucial for an evangelical in good standing, and for a Catholic, who is obliged to receive the Sacraments. We also soon discovered that he had never written anything about his supposed fundamentalist Christian beliefs, did not quote

Scripture, and was within hours of investigation shown to be the most eccentric Christian fundamentalist in the history of Christian fundamentalism. But facts should never be allowed to get in the way of a good story, and doubly so when the story centres on evil Christians. Indeed, in his personal manifesto the killer wrote:

Regarding my personal relationship with God, I guess I'm not an excessively religious man. I am first and foremost a man of logic. However, I am a supporter of a monocultural Christian Europe. If you have a personal relationship with Jesus Christ and God then you are a religious Christian. Myself and many more like me do not necessarily have a personal relationship with Jesus Christ and God. We do however believe in Christianity as a cultural, social identity and moral platform. This makes us Christian.

No intelligent person, and certainly no informed Christian, would regard this as the statement of a follower of Christ, let alone a fundamentalist follower of Christ. It's more the soggy confession of a secularist, who likes tradition and Christmas holidays, but rejects every tenet of classic Christian belief. At this stage, however, there was no stopping the journalists and the bloggers who seemed hysterically committed to blaming grotesque violence on Christians and Christianity; the folk tale of the Norwegian Christian mass murderer was firmly rooted in the psyche of mass opinion. Now, and especially then, if anybody dared to gently suggest that the real issue was the victims, and the actions of an insane man, and had nothing to do with love-based, gentleness-based, forgiveness-based Christianity, they were condemned as apologists and deniers, and even threatened and attacked. Actually, none of this came as much of a surprise, in that the same thing occurred when American right-wing extremist Timothy McVeigh carried out his deadly attack in Oklahoma in 1995, killing 165 people and injuring more than 800. He was an atheist, whose letters had repeatedly outlined his hatred for God. "Science is my religion," he'd said, and had abandoned the Roman Catholicism he had been born into many years before he became a deranged killer. He proudly told those around him that of course he did not fear Hell, because Hell did not exist. Hardly the opinion of a Christian. But he was white and Western, so he'll make do as a Christian for those whose prejudice drowns their reason.

The media did it for Breivik, they did it for McVeigh, and they do the same whenever some isolated monster attacks an abortion doctor or attacks an abortion clinic. Spend any time watching television dramas or listening to anti-Christian rhetoric, and you would assume that Christian-inspired terrorists were constantly murdering or trying to murder abortion doctors. Yet, according to NARAL Pro-Choice America, one of the most influential and vociferous pro-abortion organizations in the world,

Since 1993, seven clinic workers – including three doctors, two clinic employees, a clinic escort, and a security guard – have been murdered in the United States. Seventeen attempted murders have also occurred since 1991.

That is, of course, appalling. But it means that seven people have been killed in more than fifteen years, or one every two years. Each time such a rare incident occurs, all of the leading pro-life organizations condemn the action, offer rewards for the capture of the culprit, and join with leaders of the Protestant and Catholic churches in screaming from the spire tops that such violence is wrong, wrong, wrong! It makes very little difference to those who have already made up their minds, and whose narrative was written long ago. From a rare, intensely unusual action, they argue, we can comfortably and confidently construe that Christians are dangerous, to be feared, and are always just one step away from violence and death.

How radically different all of this is from when attacks are committed by Muslims, in the name of Islam, with the vocal support not only of millions of Muslims, but of numerous Islamic leaders, including leading and senior theologians and clerics. It is estimated that more than seventeen thousand jihadist attacks have been successfully carried out or attempted since the September 11, 2001, atrocity, most of them on fellow Muslims in the Islamic heartland of the Middle East and Asia; almost every time such an attack occurs, we hear the same arguments: that all of this is more about poverty and injustice than it is about Islam and the Koran, and that the "Christian" world is rushing to judgement. We even hear that this massive number is vastly exaggerated, which exposes an ironic racism within so many allegedly liberal and progressive people who write and broadcast in the Western world; what they mean is that there have not been seventeen thousand attacks in Europe and North America! Quite so. Most of the murders have been committed, as already explained, in the Middle East, Asia, Africa, and other parts of the developing world, and most of the victims are other Muslims. It is the nature, theology, and ideology of the perpetrator, not of the victim, that should concern us.

These same self-appointed experts and guardians of the moral conscience within mainstream, supposedly responsible, media also make every effort to qualify or disguise the words Muslim or Islamic. The killers are jihadist, Islamist, militant, or extremist. Indeed, to directly call them Muslim or Islamic is seen as being so politically incorrect as to provoke waves of angry letters and complaints to various editors and control boards, and even reprimands, suspensions, or dismissals. Large media corporations such as the BBC steadfastly forbid their reporters to refer to "Islamic" or "Muslim" terrorism, in spite of what the terrorists themselves would rather we said and believed. On the one hand, we have a passionate, perennial explanation that evil is committed by Christians, juxtaposed with an aching refusal to ever link Islam with violence and terror. And these journalists tend to be the same people who accuse more con-servative reporters of being extreme and unfair.

In the field of comedy, surely a little extremism and unfairness can be forgiven, as long as you're funny. But there are many contemporary comics who are not only unfunny, but consider themselves important shapers of political opinion through what they falsely assume to be their satire: a satire that makes of Christianity a constant whipping boy. Why? That's easy. It provokes easy and cheap laughs from people who cannot or dare not think outside of their own padded box. Comedian Bill Maher's grotesque hatred of religion has made him a lot of money, and a hero of the mindless classes. In 2008, he discussed a polygamous Mormon cult in Texas, and com-pared it to Roman Catholicism:

Whenever a cult leader sets himself up as God's infallible wingman, here on Earth, lock away the kids. Which is why I'd like to tip off law enforcement to an even larger child-abusing religious cult. Its leader also has a compound, and this guy not only operates outside the bounds of the law, but he used to be a Nazi and he wears funny hats. That's right, the Pope is coming to America this week and ladies, he's single! Now I know what you're thinking: Bill, you shouldn't be saying that the Catholic Church is no better than this creepy Texas cult. For one, altar boys can't even get pregnant. But really, what tripped up the little cult on the prairie was that they only abused hundreds of kids, not thousands, all over the world. Cults get raided, religions get parades. How does the Catholic Church get away with all of their buggery? Volume, volume, volume!

Imagine for a moment if something like this had been said about Jewish people, homosexuals, or people of colour. Remember, more than 85 percent of the victims of the tiny number of Catholics priests who were abusive were teenage boys, and their abusers were homosexual men, many of whom were also having sex with other adult men. But no Christian comic, and no comic in general, would or should make wild, cruel, inaccurate generalizations about gay people because of this, and certainly not for a cheap laugh. Actually, they wouldn't receive a laugh at all, and would doubtless lose their careers. Indeed, many journalists and performers in North America and Europe have lost their jobs for making even marginally critical comments about minority groups, some of them deservedly so because they have been ugly and wrong, but others merely because they were correct and irksome. Maher, of course, is far from atypical, and much of his and others' anti-Christian material is merely crude and scatological. These comics run in fear from mocking other faiths, ideologies, and political and sexual causes for a whole variety of reasons, but have no trouble attacking Christianity and the Catholic Church.

Yet it all goes much further than mere comics. "I make fun of Christianity, therefore I am." The credo of the liberal, the atheist, the agnostic, the trendy, the dinner-party *poseur*, the journalist, the activist, the student, the fool who merely follows the times. There are lies told and propagated, and myths accepted and encouraged about all sorts of ideologies, religions, people, and philosophies. Some of them are largely harmless, but others are aggressively damaging. Sometimes the strength or security of the victims makes the dishonesty innocuous or even irrelevant: while, for example, it might be historically irritating to believe something untrue about Napoleon III or the Treaty of Blois, or plain dumb to misunderstand the genuine teachings of Buddhism or syndicalism, it doesn't really change the way we treat others and influence the manner in which people are obliged to conduct their lives. This is not the case with some of the various ideas, individuals, and beliefs that have enormous contemporary resonance. Words have consequences. It is one of the reasons we have laws of libel and slander, so as to protect the reputations and by extension the well-being and integrity of various men and women who might otherwise suffer. Unfortunately, they may be fluffy celebrities who are merely trying to take advantage of access to lawyers, and want to protect their reputations, but they can also be significant figures who are open to all sorts of public abuse and media dishonesty. Even so, we can be too protective of feelings.

Ideologies and religions come into a different category. Things are said, for example, about capitalism, neo-conservatism, socialism, or liberalism that are absurd and hurtful. It can lead to shouting and arguing, or to anti-intellectualism and a closing of the mind. Sometimes it can be far worse, as for leftists and left-wing sympathisers who lost their jobs in the United States in the 1950s – although this phenomenon has been massively exaggerated, and some of those who did indeed lose their jobs supported an authoritarian regime in Moscow that murdered and incarcerated far more people than even that moral gargoyle Hitler. Forty and fifty years later we have conservatives being denied work in education, entertainment, and elsewhere. Attacks on an ideology can also be quite sinister: terms such as "Zionist" being used as a euphemism for "Jew," and as a consequence disguising gutter anti-Semitism and enabling it to morph into an allegedly progressive political creed. The list goes on, and there are any number of people, and all sorts of religious people, who could claim to have been repeatedly caricatured.

Yet I would argue, and I believe that the evidence is overwhelmingly on my side, that Christianity is the main, central, most common, and most thoroughly and purposefully marginalized, obscured, and publicly and privately mis-represented belief system in the final decades of the twentieth century and the opening years of the twenty-first. Islam was hardly known about beyond the obvious in general circles in the West until the mass terror attacks of 9/11, but since then there has been a distinctly divided approach. While some have tried to paint the Muslim faith as being universally violent and intolerant, these are relatively few and generally powerless. Far more common is what we are told is the considered, balanced analysis, where commentators are at pains to point out the nuances of Islam, and how it is misunderstood and treated unfairly. Much of this is the product of the Western guilt industry, and an obsession with supporting anything that seems critical of Christianity, and

Western and especially American interests. It is always stunning how some people will work so hard to justify or explain one of a plethora of grotesque episodes of violence committed by Muslims specifically and explicitly in the name of Islam, but will blithely blame Christianity for some horror performed by someone with only the most tenuous link to the Christian religion, and sometimes by people who are actually anti-Christian but happen to have been born in a vaguely Christian country.

If anyone doubts that such concerted attacks on Christianity occur, the chances are that they are not Christian, have various biases, or simply don't get out very often. It's rather like the white person from the suburbs who argues that anti-black racism is long dead. No, it's not, it's just that they have never experienced it, and lack the empathy to realize that it's out there. As for the anti-Christian attitudes, for many of us, we can take it, even though we shouldn't have to. But sometimes, in fact often, the victims of this anti-Christian campaign are the most vulnerable. In 2009, in Lexington, Kentucky, for example, a group of young teenagers at East Jessamine Middle School were treated in a way that almost defies belief. The website *beliefnet* gave what, according even to other commentators from the non-religious media, is an objective and balanced account:

֍ The mother of a student who attends the school was killed in a tragic accident. Many students gathered at school the next day between classes to pray for the family. Some teachers told the students to stop praying immediately. At lunchtime, students gathered to pray again. Someone from the school called the police and officers arrived at the school to investigate. Some students who prayed between classes and during lunch were called to the principal's office and told that prayer was not allowed at the school. After many students and parents complained, and the local news media began to investigate what had happened, the school decided the next day to allow the students to pray. Some teachers stated that the students should not have been allowed to pray on campus, however, and it is unclear whether student-led, student-initiated prayer will be permitted in the future.

If this were a unique, or even relatively isolated case, it would be irrelevant in the greater scheme. Sadly, it is far from being so.

In peaceful, traditionally tolerant, and self-consciously pluralistic Canada, to give another example, there have been numerous attacks on Christians and Christianity, often supported by state-funded and state-empowered human rights commissions. Take the case of Scott Brockie, a quiet, generally apolitical, gentle man who runs a medium-sized printing firm in Ontario. In the late 1990s, he was approached by some people who asked him to print explicit and political material from a gay organization. He explained that he was an evangelical Christian, and that while he had gay clients, the issue here was not the sexuality of the client, but the nature of the material he was being asked to reproduce. He gave the activists the names and telephone numbers of other printers in the area who would be only too happy to take their money and print their material, so that nobody would be inconvenienced. It all seemed to be a moderate compromise, satisfying to all. But no. Brockie was taken to a government-backed and -financed human rights commission, ordered to print the material, and fined several thousand dollars for not doing so when he was first asked. More than a decade later, he was told to pay $40,000 in legal fees to the Gay and Lesbian archive and the human rights commission, was given a $5,000 fine, and has now spent almost $100,000 in legal costs defending himself – the human rights commissions in question do not give any legal or financial aid to the person answering a complaint.

And those answering complaints are so often Christians! Also in Canada, but a couple of thousand miles away in a Knights of Columbus hall in British Columbia, the Knights inadvertently rented their property to a lesbian couple for their marriage party. Homosexual marriage runs directly contrary to Roman Catholic teaching, and once the Knights of Columbus discovered that the event was a gay union, they apologized for any inconvenience and agreed to find another location and to pay for new invitations to be printed. Once again, it was not enough. The men in the Knights of Columbus, who spend most of their time raising money for local charities, were taken to the province's human rights commission.

Christian activist Mark Harding was convicted in Ontario of a hate crime because he distributed leaflets to Muslims condemning Islamic violence and calling on Muslims to become Christian. He was never violent or physical – even though he himself was spat at and threatened – and he called for peace and love. Yet he was convicted, by the courts this time, ordered to perform community service, and now has a criminal record, and cannot enter the United States. In the same town, Muslim groups regularly hear sermons calling for death and conquest, yet no hate crimes charges have been laid and no arrests have so far taken place. Nor should they, of course. A crime is a crime, and hatred should not be considered a crime.

On the other side of the Atlantic, in the United Kingdom, there is no separation of church and state, but an increasingly vehement campaign against Christianity. The Archbishop of

York, Dr. John Sentamu, a black African originally from Uganda and a man who understands the reality of suffering and racism more than most, has termed the phenomenon "a campaign of mounting persecution." In 2009, to give one of many possible examples, according to Britain's *Daily Mail*,

> A school receptionist faces the sack after seeking the support of Christian friends when her five-year-old daughter was scolded for talking about God in class. Jennie Cain's daughter Jasmine was ticked off by a teacher for discussing Heaven and Hell with a fellow pupil and came home in tears. After comforting her distraught daughter, Mrs. Cain, who works at the school, sent a private email to ten close Christian friends asking them to offer prayers for the families and the school. But a copy fell into the hands of Gary Read, headmaster at Landscore Primary School, in Crediton, Devon. Now Mrs. Cain, 38, is being investigated for professional misconduct for allegedly making claims against the school and staff members. She may be disciplined and even faces dismissal. The case has caused fresh outrage in the Christian community, which fears its members are becoming the most discriminated against people in society.

In the same year in Britain, a Christian nurse, Caroline Petrie, was suspended from her job for offering to pray for a patient's recovery. The BBC, hardly a friend of Christianity, reported:

> The patient complained to the health trust about Mrs. Petrie, who follows the Baptist faith. She was suspended, without pay, on 17 December and is waiting to find out the outcome of her disciplinary meeting. . . . Mrs. Petrie, who carries out

home visits in North Somerset, said she had asked the patient if she would like a prayer said for her after she had put dressings on the woman's legs. The patient, believed to be in her 70s, refused and Mrs. Petrie insists that she left the matter alone. The sick woman contacted the trust about the incident and Mrs. Petrie was challenged by her superiors. Mrs. Petrie said: "The woman mentioned it to the sister who did her dressing the following day. She said that she wasn't offended but was concerned that someone else might be. I was spoken to by my manager. She said, "I've got a letter in one hand and an incident form in the other. You won't be able to work until we've investigated this incident." Mrs. Petrie, who qualified as a nurse in 1985, said she became a Christian following the death of her mother. "My faith got stronger and I realised God was doing amazing things in my life. I saw my patients suffering and as I believe in the power of prayer, I began asking them if they wanted me to pray for them. They are absolutely delighted." A spokesman for North Somerset Primary Care Trust said: "Caroline Petrie has been suspended pending an investigation into the matter."

Britain has also seen foster parents with outstanding records of care for some of the most unfortunate children in society losing their right to foster because of the social consequences of their Christian faith, one couple being removed from the foster list because one of the children they cared for later converted from Islam to Christianity.

In 2006, a check-in worker for British Airways at London's Heathrow Airport was suspended for wearing a small crucifix. Nadia Eweida, fifty-five, explained, "British Airways permits Muslims to wear a headscarf, Sikhs to wear a turban and other faiths religious apparel. Only Christians are forbidden to express their faith."

In 2010, Dale McAlpine was charged with causing "harassment, alarm or distress" after a homosexual police community support officer (PCSO), a part-time cop, overheard him reciting a number of "sins" referred to in the Bible, including blasphemy, drunkenness, and same-sex relationships. According to Britain's *Daily Telegraph*, McAlpine was forty-two years old at the time, and a devout Baptist, who had for some time preached his evangelical Christian faith in Workington, Cumbria, in the north of England. He was adamant then, and now, that he had said nothing about homosexuality while delivering a sermon from the top of a stepladder. But, he did admit that when a passerby asked him his views about the issue, he said that he believed homosexuality went against the word of God. The police claimed that he made the remark in a loud voice, and that it could be heard by many people in the street. He was charged by the police with using abusive or insulting language, contrary to the *Public Order Act* – which is now used quite regularly in Britain to deal with what is considered provocative comment, but was introduced in 1986 largely to deal with racist soccer thugs and far-right-wing hooligans. McAlpine was taken to a police station and held in a cell for seven hours. "I felt deeply shocked and humiliated that I had been arrested in my own town and treated like a common criminal in front of people I know," he explained. "My freedom was taken away on the hearsay of someone who disliked what I said, and I was charged under a law that doesn't apply."

The *Public Order Act*, which outlaws the unreasonable use of abusive language likely to cause distress, has been used to arrest religious people in a number of similar cases. Harry

Hammond, a pensioner, was convicted under Section 5 of the *Act* in 2002 for holding up a sign saying "Stop immorality. Stop Homosexuality. Stop Lesbianism. Jesus is Lord" while preaching in Bournemouth. Stephen Green, a Christian campaigner, was arrested and charged in 2006 for handing out religious leaflets at a Gay Pride festival in Cardiff. The case against him was later dropped.

We see similar attacks in the United States, with secularists and humanists purposely misinterpreting the reality of church-state separation, and obsessively intervening almost every time they manage to find a reference to Jesus, God, the Bible, or the Ten Commandments – not an exclusively Christian litany – somewhere on public property. Invariably, when these expensive cases occur, most people wonder why the fuss and why the expense. Do reminders of how to live our lives in moral and ethical ways, those that have made us better people for thousands of years, really do such harm when they are seen in town halls or public places, they ask? But the voice of the majority is seldom heard and rarely respected in such conflicts.

One of the most unkind and crass examples of this was when a piece of twisted iron from the 9/11 terror attacks that had mysteriously – and some argued, even miraculously – formed itself into the shape of a crucifix was to be placed in a museum to commemorate the dead of that terrible day. The campaign against this proposal began immediately. This cross must not be included, the opponents insisted, because it violates the sacred (forgive me) concept of the separation of church and state. That the majority of the first responders who died on 9/11 were Roman Catholic, and that the first such person to give his life was a Roman Catholic priest, fell on deaf ears and closed minds. Catholic League president Bill Donohue put it extremely well when he commented on the cross controversy, and on New York City mayor Michael Bloomberg's decision to ban the clergy from speaking at the 9/11 ceremony that took place on the tenth anniversary of the attack.

After the Twin Towers were leveled on 9/11 ten years ago, two steel beams in the shape of a cross were found; they were subsequently moved to St. Peter's Roman Catholic Church. Last month, when it was announced that the World Trade Center cross was being moved to its new home at the 9/11 Memorial Museum, American Atheists sued on church-state grounds to stop it. Almost everyone, including non-believers, was critical of this mean-spirited gambit by American Atheists. Among those who could not summon the courage to condemn it was Mayor Bloomberg; without criticizing these activists on moral grounds, he simply affirmed their constitutional right to sue. But when it comes to granting the clergy their constitutional right to freedom of speech on the tenth anniversary of 9/11, he does not equivocate: he simply elects to ban them. The reason given for this grand act of censorship is spurious: Bloomberg's office says the focus should be on the families who lost their loved ones. According to this logic, when the clergy are invited to speak at public events, or to open ceremonies with an invocation, they are detracting – not adding – to the overall theme. There is little doubt that if the families were asked about the propriety of allowing the clergy to speak, most would gladly say yes.

None of this, of course, compares to the persecution of Christians in the Islamic, developing, and Communist world, a cruel phenomenon that shows signs of increasing rather than diminishing. British journalist and political adviser Anthony Browne has been a business reporter and economics correspondent for the BBC, an economics correspondent, a health editor, an environment correspondent for the *Observer* newspaper, and environment editor, Europe correspondent, and chief political correspondent for the *Times*. He describes himself as a liberal democrat atheist. With this combination of vast journalistic experience and declared lack of religion considered, an article he wrote about Christian persecution is deeply significant:

> I am no Christian, but rather a godless atheist whose soul doesn't want to be saved, thank you. I may not believe in the man with the white beard, but I do believe that all persecution is wrong. The trouble is that the trendies who normally champion human rights seem to think persecution is fine, so long as it's only against Christians. While Muslims openly help other Muslims, Christians helping Christians has become as taboo as jingoistic nationalism. On the face of it, the idea of Christians facing serious persecution seems as far-fetched as a carpenter saving humanity Christianity is the world's most followed religion, with two billion believers, and by far its most powerful. . . . Across the Islamic world, Christians are systematically discriminated against and persecuted. Saudi Arabia – the global fountain of religious bigotry – bans churches, public Christian worship, the Bible and the sale of Christmas cards, and stops non-Muslims from entering Mecca. Christians are regularly imprisoned and tortured on trumped-up charges of drinking, blaspheming or Bible-bashing. Furthermore, Saudi Arabia has announced that only Muslims can become citizens.

Browne goes on to explain that Christians in Egypt are banned from numerous public offices, face regular persecution, and, although they are the original inhabitants of the country and account for between 10 and even as high as 17 per cent of the population, they are given very little influence and representation. "In the Islamic Republic of Pakistan," Browne writes, "most of the five million Christians live as an underclass, doing work such as toilet-cleaning. Under the Hudood ordinances, a Muslim can testify against a non-Muslim in court, but a non-Muslim cannot testify against a Muslim. Blasphemy laws are abused to persecute Christians. In the last few years, dozens of Christians have been killed in bomb and gun attacks on churches and Christian schools. In Nigeria, 12 states have introduced Sharia law, which affects Christians as much as Muslims. Christian girls are forced to wear the Islamic veil at school, and Christians are banned from drinking alcohol. Thousands of Christians have been killed in the last few years in the ensuing violence."

With the removal of the older authoritarian but generally anti-fundamentalist and nationalist regimes from several Arab countries during and after the so-called Arab Spring, the situation of Christians is even worse in the Middle East. Rather than being replaced by liberal and secular governments, the ruling classes in these states are now more likely to be strictly Islamic, and in Syria, Palestine, and Iraq, for example, where Christians were historically tolerated, life is becomingly increasingly difficult if not impossible for followers of Jesus. So the argument that Christians are uniquely persecuted in the opening years of the twenty-first century is really beyond dispute. Some of this new hatred is based on anger, some on neurosis, some on a misplaced self-loathing, some on mythology, some on sexual and political extremism, and much on simple lies. Lies told about Christianity and Christians.

It is my intention here to tackle just a few of the more common and most egregious of those untruths. If a lie is told often enough, it transforms itself into an ugly truth. The National Socialists taught us that. Some of the lies – there are masses of contradictions in the Bible, Jesus did not exist, Christianity has fundamentally changed its beliefs over the centuries – are simply products of ignorance and paperback wisdom. Others – Hitler was a Christian and Nazism was a creature of Christianity, Christianity is racist and encourages slavery, Christians resist progress and are frightened of science and change – are cruel deceptions, leading to social dislike and even physical violence and persecution. It is my intention in this book to deal with some of the more common lies, and reveal them to be just that. There are entire books covering some of the subjects to which I can devote only a chapter, but as a primer of logical Christian self-defence, as a handbook for followers of Christ who want to intellectualize the instinctive and provide a solid response to the increasingly malicious anti-Christian propaganda campaign, I hope this can be a guide and guard. My intention is to provide just a few metaphorical arrows, to be shot back at the snipers and the swordsmen who thrust and fire away so often. The chapters showing that Christians are far from being stupid, and have frequently led social reform, are strongly biographical, and will give readers a few large, beefy friends to walk alongside down the dark alleys and mean streets that are full of atheist bullies. They should prove to Christians they are not alone.

Some of the other chapters are more historical, such as those dealing with the reality of pagan Nazism, and the truth of the Christian response to slavery. Others are more theological and philosophical, but never so much so – I sincerely hope – that they become more wordy than worthwhile. Christianity is a living, breathing religion, and this book will succeed only if it empowers readers, who can use its contents to strengthen their faith, and to defend their faith when it is attacked. As for the atheists and assorted God-haters, some of you may perhaps rethink your position after reading the book; for those who hate the very idea of such a volume, buy it and burn it – it's very much in the atheist tradition to do so.

This is very far from being the last word, and it is certainly not even the first word. But it is the word of truth and the word of defence, in an age when truth is often the last thing that people want to read and hear. That is so terribly sad. So much so that to a good, thinking person, it is downright heresy.

I

JESUS DIDN'T EXIST AND
CHRISTIANITY IS A LATER CREATION

THIS HAD TO BE THE FIRST CHAPTER, because if Jesus did not actually live, and if basic Christian concepts and beliefs were made up much later on in history, the rest of the defence of Christianity would be a little redundant, to say the least. A warning: Because we need to establish the evidence, we need to listen to the early witnesses, and because we need to listen to the early witnesses, we need to hear them at length and in their own words. Remember, though, that what you are reading are the writings of people who were alive only a few years after Jesus walked the earth and was present here among us. We have a lot of witnesses, and a lot of evidence, which is delightfully distressing to anti-Christians when they argue that there's "just no proof." There is, and plenty of it. Whether Jesus was the Messiah is, in the final analysis, a matter of faith – though there are legions of logical arguments – but that Jesus *lived*, and that in the first decades after His life and ministry people knew what He had said and what He demanded of us, is beyond intelligent dispute. In fact, we know more about Him than we do about most other people who lived two thousand years ago, including those whose existence we take for granted and never question. It's just that it's so much less challenging to accept the historical reality of Julius Caesar or Cleopatra than it is to admit that Jesus existed.

So the denial of His existence, and the allegation that He did not do what we think He did, and did not say what we think

He said, is now incredibly common. The new atheists and the old bores tell us that to believe in Jesus Christ, in God, and to believe in the Christian religion is as intellectually *jejune* and immature as believing in Santa Claus or the Tooth Fairy. As with so many of these arguments, this one is painfully thin and illogical. Children believe in Santa Claus, the Easter Bunny, and the Tooth Fairy, but abandon these beliefs as soon as they reach the age of reason. A belief in Jesus and God, however, tends to come about *after*, not before, reaching the age of reason. Children believe in God, but they cannot understand the true significance and depth of their belief until they grow older; they come into full realization of the faith as they develop. So whereas we jettison some ideas as childish myths, we fully embrace another as adult reality. What the attack is really about, of course, is trying to discredit, abuse, and delegitimize Christianity, and to equate it with something that is self-evidently silly and not worthy of serious debate. It's very bad logic. The atheist does not believe in God, and does not believe in Santa, so God and Santa have to be equally unbelievable to a thinking person. The Christian believes in God, so he has to believe in Santa as well, and if he believes in Santa as an adult, he is a fool. This is rather like arguing that because Stalin smoked a pipe, and you smoke a pipe, you are a Communist mass murderer.

Putting all that aside, we need to respond to the fundamental accusation that there is no proof Jesus ever even existed and that Christianity and the Christian Church as we know it today is a later invention. It's one of the dumber of the attacks, but also one that some people find difficult to answer, because they assume that the people who make it know what they are talking about. Thankfully, that's not so. Let's begin very early, with Cornelius Tacitus, a Roman historian who lived in the first and second centuries. He was one of the finest historians of the ancient world, and is used today to give proof and backing to the authenticity of numerous characters and incidents from the ancient world. He said this:

> Christus, the founder of the [Christian] name, was put to death by Pontius Pilate, procurator of Judea in the reign of Tiberius. But the pernicious superstition, repressed for a time, broke out again, not only through Judea, where the mischief originated, but through the city of Rome also.

Some critics argue that Tacitus took his ideas from the Christians whom he knew, and who were biased and therefore unreliable, but this doesn't make very much sense. He was no particular friend of Christianity, and often more of an enemy; he was also an extremely reliable source, highly respected both by pagan contemporaries and by modern scholars. It's simply too convenient and facile to suddenly disregard him. There is no evidence that would lead us to conclude that this particular comment is not to be taken seriously, and if anyone had influenced him in his opinion, it would not have been a Christian but Pliny the Younger, and this strengthens rather than weakens Tacitus's commentary – more of Pliny later. It's vital to remember that Tacitus is not writing about Jesus in a positive manner, not writing as a follower or as a believer. He describes Christianity as a superstition, and as lacking the urban sophistication of Rome's various cults. It's his acknowledging that Jesus lived and died, not that He was or was not the Son of God or had any holy status, that is so significant.[1]

Gaius Seutonius Tranquillus, another noted Roman historian, also worked as a court functionary under the Emperor

Hadrian. He wrote at the end of the first century and the beginning of the second. In his evocative and compelling life of Claudius, he stated that, "as the Jews were making constant disturbances at the instigation of Chrestus, [Claudius] expelled them from Rome." This is a fascinating, and terribly sad and resonant passage full of pathos, as it refers to the suffering of the Jewish followers of Jesus, who were persecuted by both the Roman occupiers and the Jewish leadership. It shows how very early the church was established, and how much opposition there was to Christianity only a few years after the Resurrection. Some critics of this commentary have argued that the spelling – Chrestus – reveals that this is not Jesus of history who is being described, but some other local leader. Yet Chrestus was not, in fact, an uncommon variation of Jesus Christ at the time, with even noted and famous Christians such as Justin Martyr using it.

Pliny the Younger, mentioned earlier, lived between A.D. 63 and 113, and was responsible for interrogating, torturing, and executing numerous Christians because of their faith. So he was, in his grimy way, an expert on Christianity, and what he saw as its threat to Rome. He was governor of Pontus / Bithynia from A.D. 111 to 113, and wrote a whole set of letters to the emperor Trajan on a variety of political matters. The letters are extraordinary in what they reveal about the daily life of early Christianity, how individual Christians behaved, and what the pagan world thought of them and how it treated them. In one of them Pliny wrote:

> It is my practice, my lord, to refer to you all matters concerning which I am in doubt. For who can better give guidance to my hesitation or inform my ignorance? I have never participated in trials of Christians. I therefore do not know

what offenses it is the practice to punish or investigate, and to what extent. And I have been not a little hesitant as to whether there should be any distinction on account of age or no difference between the very young and the more mature; whether pardon is to be granted for repentance, or, if a man has once been a Christian, it does him no good to have ceased to be one; whether the name itself, even without offenses, or only the offenses associated with the name are to be punished. Meanwhile, in the case of those who were denounced to me as Christians, I have observed the following procedure: I interrogated these as to whether they were Christians; those who confessed I interrogated a second and a third time, threatening them with punishment; those who persisted I ordered executed. For I had no doubt that, whatever the nature of their creed, stubbornness and inflexible obstinacy surely deserve to be punished. There were others possessed of the same folly; but because they were Roman citizens, I signed an order for them to be transferred to Rome. . . .

Soon accusations spread, as usually happens, because of the proceedings going on, and several incidents occurred. An anonymous document was published containing the names of many persons. Those who denied that they were or had been Christians, when they invoked the gods in words dictated by me, offered prayer with incense and wine to your image, which I had ordered to be brought for this purpose together with statues of the gods, and moreover cursed Christ – none of which those who are really Christians, it is said, can be forced to do – these I thought should be discharged. Others named by the informer declared that they were Christians, but then denied it, asserting that they had been but had ceased to be, some three years before, others many years, some as much as twenty-five years. They all worshipped your image and the statues of the gods, and cursed Christ. They asserted, however, that the sum and substance of their fault or error had been that they were accustomed to meet on a fixed day before dawn and sing responsively a hymn to Christ as to a god, and to bind themselves by oath, not to some crime, but not to commit fraud, theft, or adultery, not falsify their trust, nor to refuse to return a trust when called upon to do so. When this was over, it was their custom to depart and to assemble again to partake of food – but ordinary and innocent food. Even this, they affirmed, they had ceased to do after my edict by which, in accordance with your instructions, I had forbidden political associations. Accordingly, I judged it all the more necessary to find out what the truth was by torturing two female slaves who were called deaconesses. But I discovered nothing else but depraved, excessive superstition.[2]

Celsus was not a Roman, but a Greek: a philosopher of the second century. He became one of the most active and thorough enemies of Christianity and Christians, having contempt for the early church but also a prescient awareness of how influential, and thus what a danger, it was likely to become. He was an authority on the religions of the Middle East, and was well versed in Jewish literature and theology. He steadfastly denied the claims of Christianity, but the significance of his writing is that he responded to what was claimed by Christians extremely early in the chronology of the Christian faith. He wrote:

Jesus, on account of his poverty, was hired out to go to Egypt. While there he acquired certain [magical] powers. . . . He returned home highly elated at possessing these powers, and on the strength of them gave himself out to be a god. . . . It was by means of sorcery that He was able to accomplish the wonders which He performed. . . . Let us believe that these cures, or the resurrection, or the feeding of a multitude with a few loaves . . . these are nothing more than the tricks of jugglers. . . . It is by the names of certain demons, and by the use of incantations, that the Christians appear to be possessed of [miraculous] power. . . .

This is extremely important. Celsus knows of Jesus's miracles, and does not even deny them as such – but tries to attribute them to sorcery or magic. Of the Virgin Birth he writes:

Jesus had come from a village in Judea, and was the son of a poor Jewess who gained her living by the work of her hands. His mother had been turned out by her husband, who was a carpenter by trade, on being convicted of adultery [with a Roman soldier named Panthera]. Being thus driven away by her husband, and wandering about in disgrace, she gave birth to Jesus, a bastard.[3]

Again, there is a clear acknowledgement here of what Christians believed was the Christian story, followed by the repetition of a libel popular at the time, and propagated by many Jewish leaders and Talmudic scholars: that Jesus's father was a Roman soldier. There is, by the way, no evidence for this, but the allegation was damning when it was said – which is why it was made – because a lack of pure Jewish blood, combined with a sexual relationship not only with a Gentile but with an occupier, was about the most venomous and condemning thing that could be said about the mother of Jesus. It's pertinent that after 1800 years of this myth being largely forgotten, it is now being given rebirth by the latest wave of atheism. We see a similar approach when Celsus writes about the Apostles, explaining that Jesus had assembled

> ten or eleven persons of notorious character . . . tax-collectors, sailors, and fishermen. . . . [He was] deserted and delivered up by those who had been his associates, who had him for their teacher, and who believed he was the savior and son of the greatest God. . . .

On whether Jesus was God or not, Celsus wrote:

> One who was a God could neither flee nor be led away a prisoner. . . . What great deeds did Jesus perform as God? Did he put his enemies to shame or bring to an end what was designed against him? No calamity happened even to him who condemned him. . . . Why does he not give some manifestation of his divinity, and free himself from this reproach, and take vengeance upon those who insult both him and his Father?

In both passages we see, again, that while Celsus doubts the Christian claims of divinity, and also sometimes doesn't know the entire truth of what was claimed, he accepts the outline of the story, because it was so well-known and accepted even by non-Christian and anti-Christian writers and witnesses.

The same is true of Lucian of Samosata, a Greek rhetorician and satirist of the early to middle second century, who was renowned for his wit and cynicism. He was one of the great political comics of his day, not to be confused with modern political comedians, who tend to stay away from dangerous targets, but, like the contemporary examples, Lucian had an obsession with Christians. He made fun of many fashions and theories of the time, but in particular Christianity, which he and many others despised as being rural, lacking in sophistication, and being at heart a religion of peasants and slaves. Yet in *The Death of Peregrinus* he writes:

> The Christians, you know, worship a man to this day – the distinguished personage who introduced their novel rites, and was crucified on that account. . . . It was impressed on them by their original lawgiver that they are all brothers from the moment they are converted and deny the gods of Greece, and worship the crucified sage, and live after his laws.

Again, we would not expect Lucian to accept and affirm Christ as the Messiah, but we see him acknowledging that the church certainly did so, and that its beliefs were widely known.[4]

Even earlier than Lucian was Mara Bar-Serapion, a stoic philosopher from Syria, who wrote a letter from prison to his son, also named Serapion. He says the following:

> What advantage did the Athenians gain from putting Socrates to death? Famine and plague came upon them as a judgment for their crime. What advantage did the men of Samos gain from burning Pythagoras? In a moment their land was covered with sand. What advantage did the Jews gain from

executing their wise King? It was just after that their kingdom was abolished. God justly avenged these three wise men: The Athenians died of hunger. The Samians were overwhelmed by the sea. The Jews, ruined and driven from their land, live in complete dispersion. But Socrates did not die for good. He lived on in the teachings of Plato. Pythagoras did not die for good. He lived on in the statue of Hera. Nor did the wise King die for good. He lived on in the teaching which He had given.

Once again, Bar-Serapion was not a Christian, but spoke of the Jewish people and their "wise king." Think of a letter written to a friend in which we describe an American president or a British prime minister. We might despise the person, and their party and politics, but we don't suddenly deny that they are president or prime minister, pretend someone else is president or prime minister, or make up an entirely false story about their opinions. It's the history, not the interpretation of that history, that matters to us here.[5]

Now let us move on to Josephus, because everybody else who writes on early Christianity does. He occupies a tremendously important place in any understanding of early Jewish history, and of the Roman world of the first century. Titus Flavius Josephus lived from A.D. 37 to 100. This Jewish priest and military leader took part in the famous but ultimately fruitless Jewish revolt against the Romans, but managed to avoid execution, became a Roman citizen, and wrote extensively about Jewish history and the period of early Christianity. In *Antiquities*, he wrote:

Now there was about this time Jesus, a wise man, if it be lawful to call him a man, for he was a doer of wonderful works, a teacher of such men as receive the truth with pleasure. He drew over to him both many of the Jews and many of the Gentiles. He was the Christ, and when Pilate, at the suggestion of the principal men among us, had condemned him to the cross, those that loved him at the first did not forsake him. For he appeared to them alive again the third day. As the divine prophets had foretold these and ten thousand other wonderful things concerning him. And the tribes of Christians so named from him are not extinct at this day.

And later in the book,

But the younger Ananus who, as we said, received the high priesthood, was of a bold disposition and exceptionally daring; he followed the party of the Sadducees, who are severe in judgment above all the Jews, as we have already shown. As therefore Ananus was of such a disposition, he thought he had now a good opportunity, as Festus was now dead, and Albinus was still on the road; so he assembled a council of judges, and brought before it the brother of Jesus the so-called Christ, whose name was James, together with some others, and having accused them as lawbreakers, he delivered them over to be stoned.

There are various beliefs among historians as to the authenticity of these passages, but it's vital that we do not throw out the early Jewish baby with the early Jewish bathwater. Some historians believe that the passages are entirely accurate, others that certain parts of them were tampered with by Christians in later centuries, but no credible historian without an obvious agenda claims that they are totally unreliable. Josephus has been used as a vital source and an essential commentator for generations, on any number of issues, personalities, and events of the first century; it would be absurdly selective and intellectually dishonest to discount him on one single subject, that being where he speaks of Jesus and Christianity.

When it comes to actual Christians speaking of Christ and Christianity, we certainly have to be more discerning about what is said and written, if not aggressively critical or even doubtful. But sometimes the evidence for the authenticity of these writings and the objectivity and accuracy of the authors is overwhelming, particularly when we realize how early they were writing and how widely read they were. Clement of Rome, for example, was killed for his Christian faith in A.D. 98. He had first-hand knowledge of the events surrounding the life, death, and Resurrection of Jesus. He wrote:

The Apostles received the Gospel for us from the Lord Jesus Christ. Jesus Christ was sent forth from God. So then Christ is from God, and the Apostles are from Christ. Both therefore came of the will of God in the appointed order. Having therefore received a charge, and being fully assured through the resurrection of our Lord Jesus Christ and confirmed in the word of God with full assurance of the Holy Ghost, they went forth with the glad tidings that the kingdom of God should come. So preaching everywhere in country and town, they appointed their first fruits, when they had proved them by the Spirit, to be bishops and deacons unto them that should believe."[6]

Ignatius of Antioch was another such Christian writer; he was made a bishop by St. Peter himself. He was a student of John the Apostle, was born just a few years after the Resurrection, and was one of the most informed of Christian writers in the first century. He was surrounded by people who knew first-hand about Jesus and His followers, and they would have been the first to criticize Ignatius if he had been inaccurate or had played the role of propagandist. Ignatius wrote:

Jesus Christ, who was of the race of David, who was the Son of Mary, who was truly born and ate and drank, was truly persecuted under Pontius Pilate, was truly crucified and died in the sight of those in heaven and on earth and those under the earth. Who moreover was truly raised from the dead, His father having raised Him, who in the like fashion will so raise us also who believe in Him.

And,

He is truly of the race of David according to the flesh but Son of God by the Divine will and powered, truly born of a virgin and baptized by John that all righteousness might be fulfilled by Him, truly nailed up in the flesh for our sakes under Pontius Pilate and Herod the tetrarch . . . that He might set up an ensign unto all ages through His resurrection.[7]

Quadratus of Athens was one of the earliest and most able defenders of Christianity, justifying and explaining his faith in the public square until his death in A.D. 126. Again, he was writing early in the history of the church, when there were numerous people in the Christian community who had seen the truth or had heard it from direct witnesses who were anxious for him to be accurate, as well as opponents of Christianity who were only too eager to pounce on any inaccuracies that he allowed to enter his writing. Quadratus stated:

> The deeds of our Savior were always before you, for they were true miracles. Those that were healed, those that were raised from the dead, who were seen, not only when healed and when raised, but were always present. They remained living a long time, not only while our Lord was on earth, but likewise when he had left the earth. So that some of them have also lived to our own times. [8]

Aristides the Athenian, a second-century Greek Christian, wrote:

> When the Son of God was pleased to come upon the earth, they received him with wanton violence and betrayed him into the hands of Pilate the Roman governor. Paying no respect to his good deeds and the countless miracles he performed among them, they demanded a sentence of death by the cross. . . . Now the Christians trace their origin from the Lord Jesus Christ. . . . The Son of the most high God who came down from heaven, being born of a pure [Hebrew] virgin, for the salvation of men. . . . And he was crucified, being pierced with nails by the Jews. And after three days He came to life again and ascended into heaven. His twelve apostles, after his ascension into heaven, went forth into the provinces of the whole world proclaiming the true doctrine. . . . They who still observe the righteousness enjoined by their preaching are called Christians. [9]

Justin Martyr was a Christian saint of the early second century, and one of the most celebrated and best-known champions of the faith in early Christianity. He was born in what is known today as Nablus, very close to the towns and villages where Jesus walked and worked. He was initially a pagan, became a Christian, and was eventually beheaded for his beliefs. He is celebrated as a saint in both the Roman Catholic and Eastern Orthodox Churches. Two passages from his writing, much of which is lost, are worth quoting here.

There is a village in Judea, thirty-five stadia from Jerusalem, where Jesus Christ was born, as you can see from the tax registers under Cyrenius, your first procurator in Judea. . . . He was born of a virgin as a man, and was named Jesus, and was crucified, and died, and rose again, and ascended into heaven. . . . After He was crucified, all His acquaintances denied Him. But once He had risen from the dead and appeared to them and explained the prophecies which foretold all these things and ascended into heaven, the apostles believed. They received the power given to them by Jesus and went into the world preaching the Gospel.

And,

At the time of His birth, Magi from Arabia came and worshipped Him, coming first to Herod, who was then sovereign in your land. . . . When they crucified Him, driving in the nails, they pierced His hands and feet. Those who crucified Him parted His garments among themselves, each casting lots. . . . But you did not repent after you learned that He rose from the dead. Instead, you sent men into the world to proclaim that a godless heresy had sprung from Jesus, a Galilean deceiver, whom was crucified and that His disciples stole His body from the tomb in order to deceive men by claiming He had risen from the dead and ascended into heaven.[10]

Finally, Hegesippus, another early second century Christian, and – important this – a convert from Judaism. He was a linguistic scholar, who spoke many Semitic languages. He wrote:

This man [James] was a true witness to both Jews and Greeks that Jesus is the Christ. . . . The Corinthian church continued in the true doctrine until Primus became bishop. I mixed with them on my voyage to Rome and spent several days with the Corinthians, during which we were refreshed with the true doctrine. On arrival at Rome I pieced together the succession down to Anicetus, whose deacon was Eleutherus, Anicetus being succeeded by Soter and he by Eleutherus. In every line of bishops and in every city things accord with the preaching of the Law, the Prophets, and the Lord.[11]

I could continue to quote from such writers for the entire book, and indeed there are such books, and many of them. Both supporters and opponents of Jesus Christ and Christianity were certain that He lived, and that the earliest followers of Christianity believed what Christians believe today. Some people at the time of the early church embraced these Christian beliefs, others detested and rejected them. But they agreed about what Christianity was and what it claimed. It would be so much simpler for anti-Christians if the story could be extinguished at the first spark, but this option isn't open to them. Instead, they try another approach. In fact, they try lots of other approaches.

THERE IS NO GOD, BAD THINGS HAPPEN TO GOOD PEOPLE, AND SO ON

WE FIND IT DIFFICULT TO DENY JESUS EXISTED, so we throw in the good old classic question, the inevitable comment, the predictable attack on Christianity that runs along the line of why would a God who is all-good, all-knowing, and all-powerful allow bad things to happen to good people? We've all heard it numerous times, and it doesn't get any more convincing on the hundredth or thousandth asking. Actually, we can just as well turn the word order of the question around and ask why an all-good, all-knowing, and all-powerful God would allow good things to happen to bad people? After all, while seeing good people suffer is horrible, it's not much fun seeing evil people having fun. It has to be said, though, that this question is sometimes asked in all innocence, by people with a genuine desire to understand what seems impossible to understand. Or it is asked by people who have themselves suffered or whose loved ones have known grief and loss. How could God let this happen to me and to mine, why would God not stop this pain and help me? At its most severe, it can be devastating. The Holocaust, the abduction and murder of a child, the long and painful death of a kind and gentle person. The critic of Christianity would respond that God is either not all-knowing, not all-powerful, or not all-good. Which, of course, implies that God exists in the first place. I would say that the question and even the problem are actually more of a difficulty and a conundrum for the non-believer than for the Christian.

The materialist and the atheist, those who would deny God, believe that at death all is over. Life is finished, it is done and complete; we are dust, mere food for worms. To these people, pain has no meaning at all other than what it is: pure, unadulterated suffering, without any redeeming purpose. There may to the atheist be a certain formless heroism attached to the person who faces suffering with courage and without complaining, but if we are all body and flesh, and no soul and spirit, if we are mere products of a selfish gene and nothing more, one wonders why this heroism would in any way be significant. There is, though, a greater point, and that is that the atheist is convinced that these years we spend on earth – perhaps 80 or 90 if we are lucky, and only a handful if we are not – are everything we have, and constitute the total human experience. Christians, on the other hand, believe that these years on earth, while important and to be used wisely and also to be enjoyed, are a preparation for a far greater life to come. They are, in effect, a thin ray of light from the great sunshine that is eternity and life in heaven with God. *My end*, as Mary Queen of Scots had it, *is my beginning.* And her end was at the sharp point of an axe, as she was beheaded on the orders of her cousin, Queen Elizabeth I. Queen Mary was certain that there was an existence beyond that on earth, as have been myriad Christians since the time of Christ. While it is neurotic rather than Christian to welcome suffering, and no intelligent and comprehending Christian would welcome suffering for its own sake, the Bible actually makes it quite clear that faith in Jesus Christ and in Christianity does not guarantee a good life, but a perfect eternity. Indeed, there is more prediction in Scripture of a struggle, and perhaps a valley of fear, on earth for the believer than there is of gain and success. There may be Christian sects that promise material wealth and all sorts of triumphs in exchange for faith, but this is a non-Christian, even an anti-Christian bargain, and has never been something that mainstream and orthodox Christianity would affirm. Christians believe that this life on earth is only the land of shadows and that real life hasn't yet begun. So yes, bad things happen to good people.

Some might argue that Christian belief is merely an excuse to escape the harshness of reality, but that is no more reasonable than arguing that atheism is a mere excuse to escape the harsh reality of judgement, and the thought of an eternity spent without and away from God. The more important point, though, is that the oft-repeated criticism that bad things happen to good people says nothing at all about God, but everything about human beings. Pain may not be desirable, but it is only a feeling, as is joy. Yet pain is not mere suffering, but also a warning sign and a way to protect us against danger. That something may hurt is undeniable, and that we will all feel some sort of pain at some point is inevitable, but whether this pain is our doing or God's is something entirely different. The all-knowing, all-powerful, all-good God allows us to suffer, just as He allows us all sorts of things, because we have the freedom to behave as we will. But He has also provided a place with the greatest contentment we can imagine if only we listen to Him, listen to His Son, and listen to His church. As to the specific issue of pain and suffering, C.S. Lewis, who watched his beloved wife die of cancer, put it this way: "But pain insists upon being attended to. God whispers to us in our pleasures, speaks in our conscience, but shouts in our pains: it is His megaphone to rouse a deaf world." God's plan is for us to return to Him, and to lead the best possible life on earth; sometimes we need to be reminded of our purpose, and pain is a sharp, clear tool to achieve that purpose. A needle may be necessary to prevent disease or infection; nobody welcomes or enjoys the injection, but it prevents a far greater suffering, just as what may seem like even intolerable pain now will lead to far greater happiness later.

Lewis also wrote:

> By the goodness of God we mean nowadays almost exclusively His lovingness. . . . By Love, in this context, most of us mean kindness – the desire to see others than the self happy; not happy in this way or in that, but just happy. What would really satisfy us would be a God who said of anything we happened to like doing, "What does it matter so long as they are contented?" We want, in fact, not so much a Father in Heaven as a grandfather in heaven – a senile benevolence who, as they say, "liked to see young people enjoying themselves" and whose plan for the universe was simply that it might be truly said at the end of each day, "a good time was had by all."

Today this applies far more obviously even than when Lewis was working and writing – he died in 1963. If I want something, runs the modern idiom, I need something; and if I need something, thus I must have something. To the Christian, however, God knows our needs better than we do, and also knows that our wants and our needs are distinctly different phenomena. Which leads to the challenge of why God would allow us to go and do wrong, and to want something that is not necessarily to our eternal advantage, or even to our immediate good.[1]

We have freedom, and we have free will. We have that free will because God, according to the Christian, is love, and no lover would allow anything else. A man who locks his wife away in a room, even if he does so for what he believes to be motives of kindness and devotion, is not a lover but an abuser, and a parent who is so protective of a child that the youngster is never allowed to leave the house will, even for what they consider the best of reasons, cause untold psychological damage to that young person. I always remember when our first child, a son, was around twelve years old, and attended a school a few miles from where we lived. We had driven him to school each day, but it was now time for him to take public transit. We worried about letting him go off alone in the crowded and, frankly, sometimes dangerous big city. But it was time, it was the right time. Off he went. And there was me, waiting at the end of the day, sitting by the door, anxious to see him come home. When he did – totally ignoring me beyond a perfunctory teenage grunt of acknowledgement – which is the way it ought to be – I was so incredibly happy and relieved. My wife and I had to let him go, but we were so relieved when he returned. Imagine, then, how God feels when we return home to Him. He lets us go, He sets us free, He acts as a loving father does, but He so much wants us home again. I was so happy when my son came home. That God allows us freedom, and sometimes a freedom to disobey, says everything about God's love for us, and nothing against it.

Yet while He wants us to return to Him, He does not force us to take this course of action, and if we choose an eternity without Him, what we have chosen is Hell. This is important, because a lot of people purposely or accidentally misunderstand the concept. Hell is not so much a place of punishment, as a place where we do not know and do not see God. We are creatures made in His image, made to love Him and to be loved by Him, and our vocation after this sojourn on earth is to be united with our maker in heaven. But we have a choice. We have freedom, we have the right to choose, even the right to choose to do the wrong thing. God in His ultimate love even gives us the right to choose not to return to Him, and to choose to spend eternity without Him, in a place we call Hell. So atheists scream at a God in whom they do not believe, for allowing them to reject Him in whom they do not believe, for allowing them to spend the rest of eternity in a place without Him in whom they do not believe. It's all a little odd and contradictory. The pain that must occur in heaven when we reject God and choose to live in a Godless place is beyond our comprehension, but this freedom of choice proves God's love and not His indifference.

Nor is it the case that He makes Himself difficult to find, which leads to the accusation that a truly good God would make it easier, even inevitable and unavoidable, that we would all follow Him and find our way to heaven. But this reveals a fundamental misunderstanding of God's involvement and intervention in history, and – again – of what choice is all about, and how enmeshed love and choice always have to be.

On the one hand, if He made Himself entirely obvious, only a fool or a masochist would purposely reject Him, and He would effectively be giving us no choice at all. Intimidating as it may seem, we are also being tested, and judged – and judgement is the last thing that modern, Western humanity is willing to be subjected to. But remember that that same modern, Western person often complains about fairness, or lack of same. It would be horribly unfair if anybody and everybody, irrespective of their choices, spent eternity in joy and completeness with God in heaven. So the same people who complain about bad things happening to good people would now loudly protest that it was wrong that such good things – actually the best things possible – should happen to bad people, some of them the worst people possible.

On the other hand, if He made Himself almost impossible to find, God would be playing cruel games with us and would be loveless, like some supreme vivisectionist, possessing power but showing no affection and without any responsibility. So He makes Himself entirely recognizable and attainable, if we have the slightest inclination to find Him. He sent us monarchs, prophets, martyrs, signs and symbols, miracles, and finally His son, to die in agony for us and then through the Resurrection prove God's love, power, and being. Not a bad set of clues when you think about it. If you think about it. But you do, yes, have to think about it.

So why do people think about it? Seriously, why do people think so much about God, including those who claim to hate Him, or more commonly, to be indifferent to Him? Think of the little boy in the classroom who pulls the little girl's hair, ostensibly because he doesn't like her or doesn't care about her. Actually, as we know, he thinks about her all the time, because in his little, unformed, and charmingly immature way, he loves her. I've often wondered why there are so many books written by atheists, so many television programs made, and so many words expressed. If He doesn't exist, if there is no God, it would surely be more sensible and logical to spend your time writing and obsessing about something else, perhaps about something that does exist. But, they might counter, we need to talk so much and so often because we need to help and liberate the other people (atheists often feel the need to educate all of the people they think are stupid and beneath them), because those other people are ignorant of the truth. These wretched people, insist the atheists, have invented God because they are weak and needy. Well, it could be true. Sure, God could be an invention, concocted by the weak and needy to help them though their sad lives. Then again, the absence of God, the non-existence of God could be an invention. It could be something invented by scared and threatened people who are too weak and needy to follow His laws and are terrified of His judgement. British playwright Tom Stoppard, not known for being a Christian or for defending God or faith, wrote in his usual pithy and delightful way that atheism is a crutch for those who cannot bear the reality of God, while the strongly Christian novelist and children's author George Macdonald wrote in the nineteenth century with great insight, "How often we look upon God as our last and feeblest resource! We go to him because we have nowhere else to go. And then we learn that the storms of life have driven us, not upon the rocks, but into the desired haven." Yes, the critics continue, but the more intelligent we are and the more we know, the less we will feel the need for God, a god, many gods, or anything else beyond our direct knowledge and experience. We will deal with some of the great Christian minds elsewhere in this book, but I advise these critics to be extremely careful with the notion that knowledge signifies wisdom. First, some of the finest minds of all time have been Christians. Second, 1930s Germany, for example, was one of the most educated and sophisticated cultures in human history, and they created the most repugnant and immoral regime of modern times, if not in all human history. There are twits who do not believe, and there are geniuses who do, and *vice versa*. It implies nothing, but is merely a facile atheistic arguing tool used by, well, by the twits. A case in point is that it was popular among rationalist thinkers in the late nineteenth century to assume that advances in textual analysis, archaeological discovery, and science would disprove the Bible. In fact, the opposite has been the case, and virtually every time we find out something new in these fields it supports rather than challenges Scripture.

But does God exist? This question and its answers have filled libraries, but we have less than a full chapter. Still, a few arguments can be briefly made. The first involves the complex nature of where we live, and the very planet, the universe itself. Consider for a moment the size of the earth, which corresponds precisely to the enormous and various demands of layers of nitrogen and oxygen that exist around fifty miles above the planet. If earth were any larger, this amount of gas would not allow gravity to exist as it does, and if any smaller it would similarly make life impossible. Of all the planets that exist, while we can speculate that others might contain meaningful life, earth is the only one with the exact recipe of gases to guarantee such an overwhelming variety and complexity of life. The same precision applies to the planet's temperature, which is of course a direct result of the relationship between the earth and the sun. Even a minor change in distance or even of angle, either closer or further, would lead to life burning or freezing to death, or for that matter never existing in the first place. The moon is also just where it should be, just where it has to be, because if it were anywhere else its influence on ocean tides would lead to mass flooding. And that very water is essential to all life. Water seems so simple, so insignificant, but it is in fact a thing of scientific beauty and perfection. Its boiling point is extremely high, its freezing point extremely low. If it were any different, we could not survive because the various changes in temperature would kill us. It keeps us at the 98.6 degrees that our bodies demand, enabling essential nutrients and minerals to be absorbed. While more than 95 per cent of the earth's water is saltwater, the miraculous phenomenon known as evaporation transforms saltwater into clean water, fit for people and for animals to use. For the Christian, of course, there is a thirst which requires something more than mere water to quench.

The atheist will argue, and we'll get to more of this later, that water is just as much an entirely natural and God-neutral construct as everything else we see and know, and they will come to this conclusion by using their brain, or at least part of it. But what a brain it is – for all of us, and not just atheists. Just contemplate for a few moments what you are doing right now, as you read this book, as you consider the contents, as you become happy or angry at what I am saying, as you feel hungry or not as you read, or as you allow your mind to wander if I am not doing my job properly, and then feel whether it is too warm or too cold in the room or just about right. Feel the ground beneath your feet, see the shapes and colours around you, react to the smells in the place where you are reading, imagine what will happen next, or perhaps remember what happened earlier, and so on and so on. But beyond this, the brain is also keeping your body working, making sure that the organs function properly, protecting you against what might threaten you, dealing with more than sixty million messages every minute. Your ability to think about all this, reflect on it, and then speak about it to someone else – even your ability to speak at all – is all a function of the brain. This could, one supposes, be pure chance. But simply to imagine that chance made the brain is itself the product of a brain that is quite an achievement for pure chance. It can be rather difficult to believe that a great power made all of this and that miracles occur, but it is far more incredible to believe that it didn't. Who, we have to ask, is making the leap of faith: the Christian or the atheist?

But could this not simply prove that we are part of a great, glorious, magnificent accident? Our distance from the sun, the position of the moon, and the conditions on earth led to the beginning of life, the existence of humans, the complexity of the brain, and our naive belief in God and the idea that He started the whole thing. Chicken and egg, God and atheist. Which came first? I opt for God, and then the atheist, and I also believe that there is quite a lot of yolk on quite a lot of atheist faces. The Christian apologist L.T. Jeyachandran puts it startlingly well when he says that "if the macro-universe provides convincing proof that we live in a well-designed world, the micro-universe that exists in all living beings (including ourselves) adds overwhelmingly to the evidence for teleos."

Beyond this is the debate surrounding the relatively recent discoveries concerning DNA. The noted British philosopher Dr. Antony Flew, who for decades had been one of the academic world's respected atheists, was obliged to change his mind about God and creation in late 2004. He said that "Superintelligence is the only good explanation for the origin of life and the complexity of nature." It's difficult to over-estimate the ripple this sent though the atheist and secular communities, who first doubted that Flew had actually said such a thing, and then, once they knew that he had, set about accusing him of having had a nervous breakdown or even of being mentally ill.

Dr. Francis Collins was director of the Human Genome Project, established to map human DNA structure, and he said that we should "think of DNA as an instructional script, a software program, sitting in the nucleus of the cell." In was in 1953 that James Watson and Francis Crick discovered the genetic structure inside the nucleus of our cells, the genetic material DNA (the abbreviation for deoxyribonucleic acid). In the past half-century, the double-helix structure of the DNA molecule has seen scientists examine and decipher the code embedded within it, and discover a language of some three billion genetic letters. The amount of information in human DNA has been compared in size to almost four hundred large encyclopedias. Author and Christian apologist Lee Strobel puts it this way: "The data at the core of life is not disorganized, it's not simply orderly like salt crystals, but it's complex and specific information that can accomplish a bewildering task – the building of biological machines that far outstrip human technological capabilities." Indeed, it would take an enormous gulp of trust and even foolishness to believe that all of this was somehow random and unplanned.[2]

This is all very good stuff, but it doesn't give us any absolute answers to the questions of God's existence. Nor will it do so, and nor can anything or anybody else do so, because there are no absolute answers – either proving that God exists or made the world, or that God does not exist and did not make the world. If we look for definite certainties in the world of faith, we do not understand the nature of the very faith we claim to possess. We've already seen evidence of the byzantine magnificence of the world, and we are free to believe that all of this did develop in spite of and not because of God, but it becomes increasingly unavoidable that the evidence certainly points to a divine designer. To take the argument in a different direction, every effect must have a cause, and we know, whatever we believe about God and Christianity, that the entire universe and everything in it is an effect. Put simply, there has to be something that caused all of this to come into existence, something that came at the beginning, something that came first, and something that was uncaused. The more that science has discovered about the earth and the stars, the more certain scientists are that the earth had a beginning, and a moment of creation. Even Richard Dawkins was prepared to write, "We have seen that living things are too improbable and too beautifully 'designed' to have come into existence by chance."[3]

Beyond this is the moral argument, being that every culture in history has possessed some form of legal code, and that what astounds us is not how different but incredibly similar they all are. These cultures and societies might disagree about the degree and level of punishment, the way someone should be judged, and the number of times someone should be forgiven, or they might even differ on some cosmetic aspects of what is right and wrong, but for the most part every race, creed, and culture, from every part of the world and at various degrees of development and sophistication, has agreed on the fundamentals of morality. Mere self-preservation and social stability do not explain this convincingly at all.

Our old friend Richard Dawkins was once asked to deliver the Christmas lectures at Britain's highly prestigious Royal Institution – the secular world obviously appreciates irony. Dawkins told the audience,

> We are machines built by DNA whose purpose is to make more copies of the same DNA. . . . It is every living object's sole reason for living. . . . The purpose of all life is to pass on their DNA means that all living things are descended from a long line of successful ancestors . . . which can best be understood as fulfilling a purpose of propagating DNA. . . . There is no purpose other than that.

And a happy Christmas to you too. Let's give the last word to a far cleverer, funnier, and nicer British author, the Christian genius G.K. Chesterton. He died in 1936, long before Dawkins and his friends were around, which is bad news for us but good news for Dawkins. In a passage from the book *Heretics* (no relation) that could be a direct response to Dawkins's Christmas lectures, Chesterton wrote:

> In the opening pages of that excellent book *Mankind in the Making*, [H.G. Wells] dismisses the ideals of art, religion, abstract morality, and the rest, and says that he is going to consider men in their chief function, the function of parenthood. He is going to discuss life as a "tissue of births." He is not going to ask what will produce satisfactory saints or satisfactory heroes, but what will produce satisfactory fathers and mothers. The whole is set forward so sensibly that it is a few moments at least before the reader realizes that it is another example of unconscious shirking. What is the good of begetting a man until we have settled what is the good of being a man? You are merely handing on to him a problem you dare not settle yourself. It is as if a man were asked, "What is the use of a hammer?" and answered, "To make hammers"; and when asked, "And of those hammers, what is the use?" answered, "To make hammers again." Just as such a man would be perpetually putting off the question of the ultimate use of carpentry, so Mr. Wells and all the rest of us are by these phrases successfully putting off the question of the ultimate value of the human life.[4]

We might not be able to prove that God exists, but we can evidently prove that those who follow Him have far better and more convincing arguments that those who do not. It would be helpful if we could toss these good arguments at the unbelievers, but that would be uncharitable. If not flinging arguments, how about throwing a few stones, or even a giant one? Because one common argument that is essentially part of introductory philosophy, or perhaps introductory theology, is one or several variations of this: If God is all-powerful, could He create a stone that is too large and heavy for Him to lift? The problem with this argument is that it's self-defeating, and implodes upon itself. Christians don't believe that God is all-powerful in the sense that a person might think of ultimate power; God is omnipotent according to His character, not according to humanity's fallen nature and broken character. So God cannot use His power to commit evil, because it would run contrary to His character. In terms of this imaginary stone – and here is where we need to concentrate – if He can perform one contradictory act and not be sufficiently strong to lift a stone He has created, He can perform another contradictory act and lift the stone which is too heavy for Him to lift. We need to say a little more about the notion of omnipotence. Some of the greatest Christian philosophers have disagreed about God and His limitless power. René Descartes in the early seventeenth century argued that God can do the logically impossible. He gave the example of shapes – God can make a square into a circle; and numbers – God can add two and two and make five. St. Thomas Aquinas in the thirteenth century took a different approach, believing that God can do anything, including the miraculous, but cannot break the rules of logic and mathematics that He himself created. If we follow Descartes, there is no argument; in his view, God can both create a stone too heavy for Himself to lift, and also lift it – contradictions simply do not apply, and have no meaning. Aquinas argues that God can do anything that is possible, but it is impossible for God to create a stone too heavy for Himself to lift.[5]

Beyond the philosophical is the practical, which too often means the banal and the prosaic. All religions are the same, claim the critics, and none of them are true anyway. It's rather like saying that all political parties are the same, and that none of them are right, or that all ideas are the same, and none of them convincing. So atheism has no more credence than theism, and anti-Christianity no more credibility than Christianity. This is pretty poor stuff, and it is used against religion, not as a serious objection, but as a way to try to marginalize and reject Christianity. I've yet to hear someone tell a Muslim, for example, especially in an Islamic country, that their religion is just the same as everybody else's. They would face a very difficult time of it if they did, whereas in a Christian nation they would not, leading us to conclude that religions are not all the same. Opinions are different from one another, and superior or inferior to one another. A religion that teaches that non-believers should be killed is quite clearly not the same as a religion that does not, just as a religion that teaches that Jesus is the Messiah is not the same as one that does not. For those who argue that religion may be different, but result in similar if not identical actions, this does not apply either. Some religions have taught that cannibalism is acceptable or even desirable, others have traditionally insisted and continue to insist on gender superiority, and condemn to death any who slander or leave the faith, and so on. But if there are those who claim all religions are all the same because they despise all of them, there are others who make the same claim specifically because they despise only one. G.K. Chesterton put it this way: "There are those who hate Christianity and call their hatred an all-embracing love for all religions." In their attempt to devalue one, they value all. Sadly, this infects some of what we think of as ecumenical movements. It's not really equal respect for all – an illogical if well-meaning idea – but a devious way of condemning one.

Prince Charles once said that when he assumed the British throne he would change his title as Defender of the Faith to Defender of Faith. The definite article would disappear, thus removing the royal title to be supreme head of the Church of England as far as the laws of God allow. In other words, the monarch would no longer be described as the head of the Anglican Church, but instead would suddenly become the great defender of all faith. Think about this for a moment. The British monarch would defend faiths that are mutually exclusive, defend one that claims Jesus as the Messiah against another one that violently denies it; defend one that says that faith in Christ leads to salvation, against another that argues that faith in Christ leads to damnation. Prince Charles's naive old liberalism aside, it shows a greater misunderstanding of what we mean by truth. Religions are not all the same, or, to put it another way, not all religions are the same. To believe in truth necessitates, whether we like it or not in these days of pluralism, that we also believe that there are lies.

At the centre of Christianity, of course, is the belief that Jesus died on a cross in Jerusalem, and rose again in fulfilment of the Scriptures. He was dead, then He lived. Christians believe this, not as a metaphor or a symbol, but rather as literal truth. Indeed to refuse or fail to believe this means that someone is not a Christian. We can admire the ideas, teachings, and example of Jesus, but if we do not acknowledge Him as the Son of God, and believe Him when He told us that He was so, and would rise again, we dismiss Him as a fraud and a liar. C.S. Lewis referred to part of this in his brilliant *Lord, Liar, or Lunatic* argument:

I am trying here to prevent anyone saying the really foolish thing that people often say about Him: "I'm ready to accept Jesus as a great moral teacher, but I don't accept His claim to be God." That is the one thing we must not say. A man who said the sort of things Jesus said would not be a great moral teacher. He would either be a lunatic – on a level with the man who says he is a poached egg – or else he would be the Devil of Hell. You must make your choice. Either this man was, and is, the Son of God: or else a madman or something worse. You can shut Him up for a fool, you can spit at Him and kill Him as a demon; or you can fall at His feet and call Him Lord and God. But let us not come with any patronizing nonsense about His being a great human teacher. He has not left that open to us. He did not intend to.

Quite so. But let's also look directly at the Resurrection, and how anti-Christians attempt to respond to it and obfuscate or deny it.

The Christian position rests on the physical, actual, and literal Resurrection. A man coming to life again, after being executed, after being killed. It's difficult to believe, but then miracles are supposed to be difficult to believe, and if they weren't, they would not be miracles, and God would not have shown us anything that should inspire us to belief. Jesus promised His followers that He would be with them for all time, but that He would also be killed and would rise again. After His resurrection, He appeared a dozen times, to a huge number of people. His first appearance was to Mary Magdalene, then to the women returning from the tomb, then to two disciples on the road to Emmaus, then to Peter in Jerusalem, then to His disciples and other followers, and again to the two men from

Emmaus. Later, after several days, He appeared again to His disciples behind locked doors, then to seven of his disciples by the Sea of Galilee, then to five hundred believers, then to James, then to eleven disciples on a mountain in Galilee, then as He walked with his disciples along the road to Bethany, then on the Mount of Olives, and then when He ascended into Heaven. So either the Bible and Christians are wrong or lying, or we have to believe this to be true. There is no middle ground, no comfortable third way – God did not leave this option open to us. If all of the early Christians were lying, they were extremely malicious, and also extremely strange, in that many of them went on to die for something they knew did not happen. It makes no sense at all. They saw Jesus crucified and they saw Him dead, and at that point the church was in disarray and the followers of Jesus in panic. It was only after they saw Him alive again that they were willing to give all for their Messiah, to the point of martyrdom. People die for the wrong reasons, and they die for base causes, but they do not die for a lie they know to be a lie. These earliest Christians saw Jesus resurrected, and they died specifically for that, because it confirmed what He had told them and had predicted, and was the miracle of miracles. If it did not happen, they had been misled, and a misleading and dishonest leader does not inspire followers to do anything at all, let alone give their lives for Him.

If they were not deceptive themselves, perhaps they were themselves deceived. But this accusation of naiveté is a little, forgive me, naive. These were extremely worldly, experienced, hardened people, who had seen and known death on a daily basis since they were children, and knew it far better than we do today. They knew the sight, the smell, and the feel of death, but they have been accused down the centuries of falling – all of them – for what is known as the "swoon theory." Adherents of this astounding idea agree that Jesus was crucified, largely because there is simply too much evidence for anyone to seriously argue the contrary. They insist, however, that He wasn't killed on the cross, but was merely wounded, traumatized, and then fainted. He was taken down, and when He was laid out on a cold slab in a tomb, woke up, pulled Himself together, and then went to see His followers, and managed to convince them that He had been killed, and had risen again. Meaning two extremely important things: that Jesus was a liar, which runs against all of the wise, kind, candid, and beautiful statements and actions said and performed in His life up to that point; and that His followers were incredibly stupid and spectacularly gullible, and suddenly accepted without question a miracle that they had only recently refused to even contemplate.

It also demands us to believe that crucifixion was something routinely and easily survived, which really would be a miracle in itself. Dr. C. Truman Davis was a nationally respected ophthalmologist and vice president of the American Association of Ophthalmology. He studied the history and reality of crucifixions in depth, and some of his detailed description of what Jesus endured is well worth repeating and considering.

Preparations for the scourging were carried out when the Prisoner was stripped of His clothing and His hands tied to a post above His head. It is doubtful the Romans would have made any attempt to follow the Jewish law in this matter, but the Jews had an ancient law prohibiting more than forty lashes. The Roman legionnaire steps forward with the flagrum (or flagellum) in his hand. This is a short whip consisting of several heavy, leather thongs with two small balls of lead attached near the ends of each. The heavy whip is brought down with full force again and again across Jesus' shoulders, back, and legs. At first the thongs cut through the skin only. Then, as the blows continue, they cut deeper into the subcutaneous tissues, producing first an oozing of blood from the capillaries and veins of the skin, and finally spurting arterial bleeding from vessels in the underlying muscles.

The small balls of lead first produce large, deep bruises which are broken open by subsequent blows. Finally the skin of the back is hanging in long ribbons and the entire area is an unrecognizable mass of torn, bleeding tissue. When it is determined by the centurion in charge that the prisoner is near death, the beating is finally stopped. The half-fainting Jesus is then untied and allowed to slump to the stone pavement, wet with His own blood. The Roman soldiers see a great joke in this provincial Jew claiming to be king. They throw a robe across His shoulders and place a stick in His hand for a scepter. They still need a crown to make their travesty complete. Flexible branches covered with long thorns (commonly used in bundles for firewood) are plaited into the shape of a crown and this is pressed into His scalp. Again there is copious bleeding, the scalp being one of the most vascular areas of the body. After mocking Him and striking Him across the face, the soldiers take the stick from His hand and strike Him across the head, driving the thorns deeper into His scalp. Finally, they tire of their sadistic sport and the robe is torn from His back. Already having adhered to the clots of blood and serum in the wounds, its removal causes excruciating pain just as in the careless removal of a surgical bandage, and almost as though He were again being whipped the wounds once more begin to bleed.

In deference to Jewish custom, the Romans return His garments. The heavy patibulum of the cross is tied across His shoulders, and the procession of the condemned Christ, two thieves, and the execution detail of Roman soldiers headed by a centurion begins its slow journey along the Via Dolorosa. In spite of His efforts to walk erect, the weight of the heavy wooden beam, together with the shock produced by copious blood loss, is too much. He stumbles and falls. The rough wood of the beam gouges into the lacerated skin and muscles of the shoulders. He tries to rise, but human muscles have been pushed beyond their endurance. The centurion, anxious to get on with the crucifixion, selects a stalwart North African onlooker, Simon of Cyrene, to carry the cross. Jesus follows, still bleeding and sweating the cold, clammy sweat of shock, until the 650 yard journey from the fortress Antonia to Golgotha is finally completed.

Jesus is offered wine mixed with myrrh, a mild analgesic mixture. He refuses to drink. Simon is ordered to place the patibulum on the ground and Jesus is quickly thrown backward with His shoulders against the wood. The legionnaire feels for the depression at the front of the wrist. He drives a heavy, square, wrought-iron nail through the wrist and deep into the wood. Quickly, he moves to the other side and repeats the action being careful not to pull the arms too tightly, but to allow some flexion and movement. The patibulum is then lifted in place at the top of the stipes and the titulus reading "Jesus of Nazareth, King of the Jews" is nailed in place. The left foot is now pressed backward against the right foot, and with both feet extended, toes down, a nail is driven through the arch of each, leaving the knees moderately flexed. The Victim is now crucified. As He slowly sags down with more weight on the nails in the wrists excruciating pain shoots along the fingers and up the arms to explode in the brain – the nails in the wrists are putting pressure on the median nerves. As He pushes Himself upward to avoid this stretching torment, He places His full weight on the nail through His feet. Again there is the searing agony of the nail tearing through the nerves between the metatarsal bones of the feet. At this point, as the arms fatigue, great waves of cramps sweep over the muscles, knotting them in deep, relentless, throbbing pain. With these cramps comes the inability to push Himself upward. Hanging by his arms, the pectoral muscles are paralyzed and the intercostal muscles are unable to act. Air can be drawn into the lungs, but cannot be exhaled. Jesus fights to raise Himself in order to get even one short breath. Finally, carbon dioxide builds up in the lungs and in the blood stream and the cramps partially subside. Spasmodically, he is able to push Himself upward to exhale and bring in the life-giving oxygen. It was undoubtedly during these periods that He uttered the seven short sentences recorded.

The Romans were experts in many things, including in how to execute people. There is only one reliable record of a man surviving a crucifixion, but he was severely disabled after his experience, and his survival is known to us precisely because it was so extraordinary. Both the Romans and the Jewish authorities were determined that Jesus should die, His was a high-profile execution and certainly closely supervised, and even if He had not died on the cross, He would not have been able to walk, even move, after such a prolonged torture. There was also a large boulder rolled in front of His tomb, requiring two men to roll it away. Yet the Jesus who conveniently survived whipping, beating, and crucifixion, with massive blood loss and muscle and sinew damage, apparently slid this boulder away with ease, then appeared before His followers – who thought His body glorified! It would have been smashed, broken, ripped, severed, emaciated, bloody, and with exposed intestines, but the last thing it would have been was glorified. This is fantasy, from those who condemn Christians for believing in the supernatural.

If the swoon theory does not stand up to scrutiny, continue the deniers, it can all be explained by a case of mass hallucination, or groupthink, leading to a state of sensory illusion and obsessive, fantastic imagination and wishful thinking. The disciples wanted so strongly to see their master alive again, we are told, that they imagined they saw Him; one encouraged the other, and in the end they all claimed to have seen the resurrected Jesus. The problem with this scenario is that it says more about the wishful thinking of critics of Christianity than it does about that of the early Christians. Many of those who saw Him did not expect to see Him, had not heard of His prophecies, or did not want to see Him. Remember, beyond the fact that He appeared after His resurrection to ordinary men and women who were not His followers, the first people to have seen Him alive again were women, and if the original and still tiny Christian church had wanted to record some sort of group hallucination, they would certainly have put a more appealing and convincing spin on it than this – women's testimonies were not considered equal to those of men in the first-century Middle East, if taken seriously at all. Or, the argument continues, perhaps none of this happened at all, and was all part of a huge conspiracy, painstakingly constructed to give birth to a new religion. As we've already discussed, this runs against human logic and behaviour, as so many of the people alleged to have been behind the lie went on to give their lives for it.

Also consider the effort and planning involved to silence those who saw Jesus's body, and were likely to tell people that He had not risen from the dead. The Jewish leaders and the Roman government would certainly have tried to encourage and sponsor those who could prove there was no Resurrection, as this would have smothered Christianity at birth. At any time since those first few years, the showing of His body or any reasonable evidence that He did die would also have broken the Christian claim, right up till the modern age. It's actually much easier and more intellectually consistent to disregard these theories and believe the Christian claim. But that would lead to one becoming a Christian, which is the last thing an anti-Christian wants.

So if all of these attacks seem to fail, move on to the commonly encountered "the Bible is full of contradictions" approach. Actually there aren't really any contradictions, and usually when you push someone and ask for specific examples, they cannot give you any. But one of the most common, and one that is a good example of the vacuity of this argument, is taken from the Gospel of Matthew, where in the fifth chapter, Jesus says:

You are the light of the world. A city on a hill cannot be hidden. Neither do people light a lamp and put it under a bowl. Instead, they put it on its stand, and it gives light to everyone in the house. In the same way, let your light shine before men, that they may see your good deeds and praise your Father in heaven.

But in the next chapter, He says,

And when you pray, do not be like the hypocrites, for they love to pray standing in the synagogues and on the street corners to be seen by men. I tell you the truth, they have received their reward in full. But when you pray, go into your room, close the door and pray to your Father, who is unseen. Then your Father, who sees what you do in secret, will reward you.

There we have it: a contradiction. And indeed after a first and cursory look, it does seem that Jesus tells us on the one hand to keep our religious views secret, and on the other to make them public and well-known. But accuracy requires more than just a first and cursory look. Part of the problem lies in a misunderstanding of what the Bible is, and a failure to appreciate context, and to realize that a difference in emphasis or a biographical disagreement is not the same thing as an outright contradiction. Who was Jesus speaking to, what was He trying to point out to His listeners, and to what was He responding? I, for example, have written several biographies of various literary figures. When I was writing lives of H.G. Wells or Arthur Conan Doyle or J.R.R. Tolkien, I could not mention every event that occurred in these three long and illustrious lives. Instead I was, as is every biographer, selective in what I included and did not include. Similarly with Matthew, Mark, Luke, and John. They wrote brief lives of Jesus Christ, and wrote them for very different audiences. John might stress a certain aspect of the life of Christ, Luke might stress another, but differences in interest and concentration do not produce a contradiction. Some of them even differ about dates and places, and details of what happened, but none contradict each other about the crucial events in the life of Jesus. Or, and this is fundamental, deny that He was the Son of God.

The alleged contradiction in Matthew is helpful rather than hurtful because it allows us to clarify this entire problem. In chapter 5, Jesus is discussing our good deeds, but in the next chapter He is referring to our beliefs and devotions. When you perform a good deed, Jesus tells us, you do not boast of it so as to claim praise and prestige for yourself, but only allow it to be known because it reflects on you as a believer, and demonstrates what your relationship with God has encouraged you to do and achieve. It's not about self-glorification, but the glorification of God, and this light on the hill will encourage others to follow you in goodness and faith, and pleases God. Beware of false modesty, He tells us, and the paradoxical pride of hiding goodness out of a feeling of self-aggrandisement. The second passage, on the other hand, speaks of prayer and how we speak to and praise God. Because prayer is at heart a personal communication with God, where we speak to and listen to Him, we do not need to make it public, and if we do so, there is a danger that we are praying, not to commune with God, but to show other people that we are holy and devout, leading to ourselves rather than God being admired. It's quite straightforward if we give it some time and thought.

These attacks, the theories, and the denials are legion, and whenever anyone tells me that they have a new argument against Christianity I always tell them that they haven't. Believe me, I've heard them all before. Yet while the criticisms of the faith are many, the rational and effective responses are even greater. In the past, we could win an argument and change minds, but today if we win an argument, people tend to simply walk away. Truth has far less importance in Western culture than it did. Sometimes truth is distorted, wrapped in fiction and fantasy, and even sells millions of books. Sometimes it's called *The Da Vinci Code*.

▮▮▮

THE DA VINCI CODE

IT HAS TO BE TRUE, because I read it in *The Da Vinci Code*, or I saw it in the movie. With apologies to Winston Churchill: Never in the field of human thinking has so much harm been done to so many by such a bad author. Leaving aside for a moment the direct Christian response to the book, we ought to remember that many reviews in the intelligent press were downright awful. In giving his opinion of the movie of the book in the far from pro-Christian *New Yorker*, National Magazine Award–winning writer Anthony Lane summed up the book bitingly well:

> There has been much debate over Dan Brown's novel ever since it was published, in 2003, but no question has been more contentious than this: if a person of sound mind begins reading the book at ten o'clock in the morning, at what time will he or she come to the realization that it is unmitigated junk? The answer, in my case, was 10:00.03, shortly after I read the opening sentence: "Renowned curator Jacques Saunière staggered through the vaulted archway of the museum's Grand Gallery." With that one word, "renowned," Brown proves that he hails from the school of elbow-joggers – nervy, worrisome authors who can't stop shoving us along with jabs of information and opinion that we don't yet require. . . .
>
> Should we mind that forty million readers – or, to use the technical term, "lemmings" – have followed one another

over the cliff of this long and laughable text? I am aware of the argument that, if a tale has enough grip, one can for a while forget, if not forgive, the crumbling coarseness of the style; otherwise, why would I still read *The Day of the Jackal* once a year? With *The Da Vinci Code*, there can be no such excuse.[1]

Meaning that Mr. Lane may well be assassinated by a mad albino monk working for Opus Dei! The fatuous and risible *Da Vinci Code* has caused incalculable problems, and even convinced admittedly flimsy Christians to abandon their faith. I remember being on vacation in England – the country of my birth and upbringing – and taking a friend to the beautiful and historic Temple church in London. There was a visibly frustrated and almost angry tour guide pointing to a printed sign at the front of the church, explaining to her group that *The Da Vinci Code* was not authentic or reliable, and that the people on the tour should stop asking her questions about the novel, and instead enjoy and appreciate the ancient building in which they were standing. Enjoy it, that is, for what it is and was, and not for what it is not and never was. The book, the movie, and even the board game. No joke. There really is a *Da Vinci Code* board game. Roll a double six, proceed five squares and then beat oneself with a whip while murdering a nun. Christians are doing a pretty good job of turning the other cheek.

The Islamic world went into mass revolt over a bunch of largely innocuous cartoons depicting the prophet Mohammad and killed many innocent people; it promised death to unbelievers and promised to decapitate the Pope following his repetition of a remark about Islam made at the end of the fourteenth century by Manuel II Palaiologos, the Byzantine emperor; and it generally screams, threatens, and kills if it feels Islam is being insulted in any way whatsoever. But Christians behave differently. Dan Brown writes the most repugnant things about Christianity and its followers, and the result is a few angry letters – which is probably the way it should be. But that Brown makes repugnant and completely baseless attacks on Christianity places him firmly in the centre of secularism's current obsession: the fetish of hatred against the Christian faith, the religion that stands firm against relativism, moral decay, and self-indulgence. Combine this anti-Christianity with a few beautiful heroes, a mad monk or two, some facile plots, and the now obligatory conspiracy theory, and the pages turn as fast as the figures on a certain author's bank account. A daft novel, however, is merely that. It is when Dan Brown claims to be writing fact, as he does at some length in the book, that we have a duty to correct him.[2]

Brown claims that Jesus was regarded even by His followers as merely a great moral teacher or at best a prophet. We dealt with this canard in the previous chapter. They never thought of Him as a Messianic figure, Brown continues, and the earliest written documents substantiate this. It was only at the Council of Nicaea in A.D. 325 that Jesus was said to be divine. Not quite. Jesus is called "God" seven times in the New Testament and is referred to as being divine on dozens of occasions. He was crucified, not for being a prophet or an ethicist, or for that matter a champion of social justice, but for claiming to be the Son of God. The early martyrs died because of this belief alone. There are numerous letters from pagan and thus objective writers from the first and second centuries, long before the Council of Nicaea, describing how Christians believed Jesus to be divine, including one written to the Emperor Marcus Aurelius, who died in A.D. 180. All the Council of Nicaea did was to affirm that Jesus was in fact the Son of God.

Brown then says that the Dead Sea Scrolls are the earliest Christian writings in existence and that the Gnostic Gospels frequently mention Mary Magdalene and her marriage to Jesus. This really is a howler. The Dead Sea Scrolls are Jewish writings and have no direct connection with Christianity at all. As for those much-discussed Gnostic Gospels, they at no time mention Jesus as being married to Mary Magdalene. But then Dan Brown probably doesn't expect his readers to actually read the Gnostic Gospels. If they did, they would be extremely disappointed. They are often misogynistic, are frequently contradictory, and tend to be self-serving and surprisingly dull. They were rejected by the Church because they were written relatively late and are wholly unreliable. It was not a case of Christianity trying to hide some greater truth, but of Christianity only adopting books that were, well, Christian. Brown tells his readers that many people knew that Jesus was married to Mary Magdalene, and that it was common knowledge – "Oh, did I tell you I saw that Jesus and his wife last week? They're a lovely couple, and very much in love, you know." Please! Brown says that members of the early church knew this, and that as the information became suppressed, it was only people such as Leonardo da Vinci who were let in on the secret. It all stretches credibility well beyond breaking point, but there are few so credulous as those eager to hear bad news and bad things about Christianity.[3]

Brown claims as his evidence for the fatuous marriage story two gospels that were rejected by the church when the New Testament was assembled. One is the Gospel of Mary, the other the Gospel of Philip. Oddly enough, while both state that Jesus loved Mary more than anybody else, including His twelve disciples, neither of them actually say that the pair were married. One refers to Mary as the "companion" of Jesus, the other has Jesus kissing Mary on the lips in front of other people, the assumption made by Brown being that such a public display must indicate that the two were husband and wife. The problems with all this are myriad. Most important, very few, if any, scholars take these particular gospels seriously – they were rejected by the early church precisely because they were so obviously unreliable – and their contents have been dismissed for centuries not just by Christians, but also by critics of Christianity. But even if they were to be taken seriously, they don't suggest marriage at all. The original text of the so-called kissing gospel, so vital to Brown's thesis and to others who obsess about the married Christ, does not refer to Jesus kissing Mary on the lips, largely because while a kiss is indeed described, lips are not mentioned. This is a later, and horribly tendentious, reading of the text, by agenda-driven commentators. It is far more likely, if it happened at all, to have been a kiss on the cheek, a common sign of friendship and platonic love between men and women in first-century Palestine. As for the word "companion," it could just as likely describe Jesus's relationship with all of his close followers, male and female. The assumption that it is exclusive or implies something physical, sexual, or especially intimate is at best a weak anachronism, and probably something far worse. In other words, it says nothing at all.

This modernist nonsense also says a great deal about contemporary arrogance and sloth. We're too full of ourselves to think deeply about this, and too lazy to do the leg work. The gospels quoted by Dan Brown are by and large highly questionable biographies of Jesus, written by people with no intimate knowledge of His life and ministry. There is ample pagan as well as Christian writing about Jesus from the earliest times, and what we see is that it's not just Christians who never claim that He was married, but the enemies of Christianity as well, who were anxious to discredit the new religion, and prepared to do almost anything, including lie, to smash this great threat to the established order. Even they knew that the marriage claim would be dismissed and would harm their case and credibility. Yet we don't have to look back two thousand years to be reassured that the marriage suggestion is nonsense. Since the late nineteenth century, attempts to discredit Christianity have come from numerous sources, some of them informed and impressive academics. Yet even the most intelligent, as well as the most crass and aggressive, have not seriously claimed any real evidence that Jesus was married. Today, with atheism taught in schools and universities, and even regarded as a default position, while people will say the most outrageous things about Jesus and Christianity, nobody of intellectual note has made a compelling case for the married Christ.[4]

If Brown doesn't think much of the Christian Church, he doesn't like the Emperor Constantine at all. Except when he thinks of him as a virtual god. "The Bible, as we know it today, was collated by the pagan Roman Emperor Constantine," he writes. Who knew? Certainly not Constantine. Because the Old Testament existed even before the birth of Jesus, and the New Testament began to take shape at the end of the first century. The compilation was not finalized until the end of the fourth century. Constantine, however, died in A.D. 337. In other words, there is no way that he could have compiled the Bible. What he certainly did do was to commission Eusebius, the great Bishop of Carthage, to make fifty copies of the Bible that already existed so that more people could read it. No serious historian has ever claimed otherwise or written anything to support Brown's thesis.

There is far more, however. Dan Brown tells his readers that the contents of the Bible, and the foundations of the Christian Church, were decided by a vote, and a close one at that, at the Council of Nicaea in A.D. 325. Truth cries out to be heard. As we saw earlier, the council was called, not to decide on whether God was God or Jesus the Messiah, but to respond directly to what are known as the Arian heresies – a set of beliefs that, while acknowledging that Jesus was the Son of God, stated that this was by appointment, and not something inherent from the beginning of time. It seems an esoteric and involved point, but it is in fact deeply significant. But it is not what Dan Brown claims by a very long way. Nor is he correct when he writes that Constantine assembled the council for self-ish and manipulative reasons. There were from various times 216 to 316 bishops at Nicaea, and they were brought together to make sure that the Church moved forward in unity and con-gress. They signed the Nicene Creed, with only two voices of dissent, outlining the beliefs of Christianity as we know them today. So, far from being a political gathering, told by the emperor to engineer a new, Christian belief system, the council and the creed merely solidified a collective affirmation of what was already known and believed. It was what Ignatius of Antioch in A.D. 110 said: "For our God, Jesus Christ, was conceived by Mary in accord with God's plan: of the seed of David, it is true, but also of the Holy Spirit." What Tatian the Syrian wrote in A.D. 170: "We are not playing the fool, you Greeks, nor do we talk nonsense, when we report that God was born in the form of a man." What Clement of Alexandria wrote twenty years later: "The Word, then, the Christ, is the cause both of our ancient beginning – for he was in God – and of our well-being. And now this same Word has appeared as man. He alone is both

God and man, and the source of all our good things." What Tertullian said in A.D. 210: "God alone is without sin. The only man who is without sin is Christ; for Christ is also God," and what Origen wrote fifteen years after that: "Although he was God, he took flesh; and having been made man, he remained what he was: God." All long before the Council of Nicaea in 325, and a very long time before Dan Brown's fantasies.[5]

While we know that Brown is not a historian, we also know that Athanasius certainly was one, and he tells us as early as A.D. 367 that there were twenty-seven books in the New Testament, in the same form we all know seventeen hundred years later. More than this, it is agreed on by academics and theologians, including liberal academics and theologians, that the four gospels of Mark, Matthew, Luke, and John were recognized as the only reliable, authoritative version of the life of Christ by the end of the second century, which is more than a century before the Emperor Constantine and the Council of Nicaea. We know that as early as the beginning of the third century, gospels such as those of Mary and Thomas were totally ignored, because these early Christians simply did not take them seriously and knew that they had no authority. The Church Father Origen gave a homily confirming this at the time. The reason Dan Brown has managed to convince so many people that he is privy to some exciting, hidden truth is, frankly, because of theological illiteracy. Not everybody has to be a theologian – we have far too many of them as it is, for all the good they do – but before people accept theological ideas that seem revolutionary, they should surely familiarize themselves with at least the basics of the field they claim to appreciate. Nothing Brown claims about Jesus in *The Da Vinci Code* is new, most of it is false, and some seems to be just made up. Yes, but that's what fiction is, insist his supporters. But a large part of the reason for the book's success is that Brown leaves the taste of authenticity with the reader, and more than a flavour of non-fiction. We live in the empty, needy age of the conspiracy theorist, and this is a conspiracy theory *par excellence*.[6]

And if Dan Brown does sometimes play the novelist card, and doesn't always claim that he is a historian writing truth and history, he certainly makes the case for others. "The royal bloodline of Jesus Christ has been chronicled in exhaustive detail by scores of historians," he writes. The historians he lists are Margaret Starbird, Richard Leigh, Henry Lincoln, Clive Prince, Lynn Picknett, and Michael Baigent. There is a major problem here. Just like Dan Brown, these aren't historians either. Baigent has a degree in psychology and is working on an M.A. in mysticism, and Picknett and Prince are best known for their work on the occult and UFOs. Phone home, ET, and tell us about Jesus and his family, who all live in France.

Brown is often at his most fatuous when he tries to be at his most clever. He writes that YHWH, the Jewish sacred name for God, is based on the word Jehovah. And Jehovah, he says, is a combination of the masculine Jah and the feminine Havah, signifying Eve. Thus God gave us feminism, Jesus was a pioneer of progressive gender politics, and the Church has hidden all of this to preserve male power and exclude women, particularly Mary Magdalene, from their rightful place in society and culture. Dan, you've got your politics and your semantics rather confused. YHWH doesn't come from Jehovah, but Jehovah from YHWH. The word was used thousands of years before Jehovah came into existence, which was as late as the sixteenth century. Brown goes on to say that the Priory of Sion was founded in early medieval Europe. Untrue. It was registered with the

French government in a dusty office in 1956. Even the BBC, hardly a friend of Christianity, concluded:

> There's no evidence for a Priory of Sion until the 1950s; to find it, you go to the little town of St. Julien. Under French law every new club or association must register itself with the authorities, and that's why there's a dossier here showing that a Priory of Sion filed the proper forms in 1956. According to a founding member, this eccentric association took its name not from Jerusalem but from a nearby mountain (*Col du Mont Sion*, alt. 786 m). The dossier also notes that the Priory's self-styled grand master, Pierre Plantard, who is central to this story, has done time in jail.

One of Dan Brown's central bad guys in the book is an Opus Dei monk. Yet there are no such things. The Roman Catholic group Opus Dei is an overwhelmingly lay organization and they have no monks. Opus Dei's U.S. communications director, Brian Finnerty, puts it plainly and accurately:

> The real Opus Dei was founded in Spain in 1928 by a Catholic priest, St. Josemaría Escrivá, with the purpose of promoting lay holiness. It began to grow with the support of the local bishops there and was approved as a secular institute of pontifical right by the Holy See in 1950. Opus Dei's work has been blessed and encouraged by Popes John XXIII, Paul VI, John Paul I, and John Paul II. In 1982, John Paul II established it as a personal prelature of the Catholic Church after careful study of its role in the Church's mission. The culmination of the Church's support for Opus Dei and its message came with the 2002 canonization of its

founder. Pope John Paul has called Opus Dei's founder the saint of ordinary life.

The truth is not as exciting as the Dan Brown version, but the truth isn't always what we want it to be.[7]

Brown also states that five million women were killed by the Church as witches in medieval Europe. Actually between 30,000 and 100,000 people, men and women, were executed for various crimes, including witchcraft, in the period Dan Brown describes. He also refers to the Pope being in the Vatican long before the Pope actually resided in the Vatican. Even Tom Hanks, the star of the feature film made from the book and its sequel, admits that there is a great deal of "hooey" in the movie and that people shouldn't take it all seriously. But Tom, would you act in a movie denying the Holocaust or questioning the obscenity of the African slave trade, and then justify your work because it is only entertainment? The question is rhetorical, the answer illuminating. *The Da Vinci Code* insists that evil men and women have for 2000 years been telling a grotesque lie and that they still torture and kill to maintain their power. That's pretty damning and has caused enormous pain to many good, kind people.

Perhaps the most visual, facile, and obvious falsehood given to the world by Dan Brown is that the figure next to Jesus in da Vinci's famous painting "The Last Supper" is not a man at all, but the same Mary Magdalene, who, as we've seen, was in Brown's fevered imagination married to Jesus. It's odd how the very people who like to tell us how evil Christianity is, and how anybody who contradicted Christian teaching was persecuted and tortured, also want to believe that Leonardo da Vinci blithely painted Mary Magdalene in his "The Last

Supper," knowing that the Pope and the Christian world would just congratulate him on such a nice picture and praise his joke as being even funnier than his cartoons. In fact, the figure Leonardo painted next to Jesus in that wonderful picture is John the Evangelist, the youngest of the close followers of Christ, who is always depicted in medieval and renaissance art without a beard. Note to Dan Brown – women are defined by more than the absence of a beard.

Brown has been asked whether he is a Christian, and while the answer is not directly relevant – whether Christian or not a Christian, one expects honesty – his response speaks volumes. On his official website he explained,

> I am, although perhaps not in the most traditional sense of the word. If you ask three people what it means to be Christian, you will get three different answers. Some feel being baptized is sufficient. Others feel you must accept the Bible as immutable historical fact. Still others require a belief that all those who do not accept Christ as their personal savior are doomed to hell. Faith is a continuum, and we each fall on that line where we may. By attempting to rigidly classify ethereal concepts like faith, we end up debating semantics to the point where we entirely miss the obvious – that is, that we are all trying to decipher life's big mysteries, and we're each following our own paths of enlightenment. I consider myself a student of many religions. The more I learn, the more questions I have. For me, the spiritual quest will be a life-long work in progress.

Actually Dan, that's nonsense. The most basic qualification to be a Christian is to *be a Christian*, and that means believing

Christ is the Messiah, not that He was some married fellow who said the occasional good thing.

We'd all be better off if, instead of reading Dan Brown, we read good, original, intelligent authors who have something to say about the world. Perhaps we could even read some Christian authors, but then, we are told repeatedly that the clever people, authors and the like, are not Christians.

IV

ALL THE CLEVER PEOPLE ARE ATHEISTS.
OR, CHRISTIANS ARE STUPID

IT SHOULD BE OBVIOUS THAT RELIGIOUS BELIEF is entirely distinct from intellectual status. There have been and are outstandingly clever as well as ordinary, basic, and even educationally substandard people who have been Christian, and there have been and are outstandingly clever as well as ordinary, basic, and even educationally substandard people who are non-Christian or even anti-Christian. It's a modern *canard*, a common libel, that the thinking, reading, enlightened types are always secular or atheistic. It works particularly well at universities, where teachers often, and shamefully, make it very difficult for students who are Christian to be taken seriously, and mock them to the point where they are quiet about their faith or even lose it completely. The thesis is, like so much in the atheist cosmos, a mere soufflé that evaporates with a clear, clean gust of wind. There is really no way to prove the argument, and critics who think that Christians are stupid, or at least credulous and gullible, will doubtless continue to do so. All I can do is to give a set of examples of people who were clearly intellectual giants and could have chosen any ideology, religion, or belief system they wanted, but decided on orthodox and serious Christianity. Elsewhere in the book I discuss Christian scientists and Christian reformers, but here I concentrate on Christian writers. I also concentrate on British, Christian writers. I ask forgiveness for the anglocentrism, but I am from Britain and was formed as a Christian in that country. More to the point, the fact that these writers all come from one small country illustrates the number and depth of Christian intellectuals. I could have chosen many other countries and selected just as many examples. The people chosen are all British and all authors, but they are Catholic and Protestant, poets and novelists, wrote for children as well as adults, wrote detective stories and works of theology. In other words, they are various, but have in common their devotion to Jesus Christ.

One of the greatest literary defenders of Christianity was a man quoted several times elsewhere in this book: C.S. Lewis. He liked to be called Jack. Plain Jack. It suited his character, or so he thought. Certainly those who knew him said that he looked like an ordinary high-street butcher. Until he spoke, and until he wrote. Oh, and how he wrote. *Mere Christianity*, *The Screwtape Letters*, *Surprised by Joy*, and *The Lion, the Witch and the Wardrobe*, among so many other titles. C.S. Lewis, Clive Staples, one of the finest popular communicators of the Christian message and the Christian life who ever lived. He was born in November 1898 in Belfast, Northern Ireland. Several of his Narnia books written for children have been made into movies, and commercialism being what it is, there is now a thunderstorm of books and videos. But it is a sweet rain and in this case it is a joy to be made wet. Lewis would have laughed at such antics, always seeing himself as an ordinary teacher and an ordinary Christian. In fact, he was a most extraordinary teacher. A lecturer at both Oxford and Cambridge, he was considered one of the finest minds of his generation by fellow professors. His *English Literature in the Sixteenth Century Excluding Drama* and *The Allegory of Love* are still considered academic masterpieces. But it was Lewis the Christian who changed the world. His genius was the ability to convey highly complicated and complex ideas in a straightforward and understandable manner. Like some grand knight of common sense, he charged through the ranks of cluttered thinking, double-talk, and atheism, seldom taking any prisoners.[1]

Lewis declared himself a Christian in 1929, "perhaps the most dejected and reluctant convert in all England." It was as though he had tried to avoid the inevitable, considering every argument against Christianity, forcing himself to take on all of the objections his fertile mind could produce. Each one he overcame. By the time his intellect was well and truly won over, his emotional being simply fell into place. From this point on, everything he wrote was informed and enlivened by his Christianity. But Lewis was too subtle and too clever to knock people over the head with his faith. He knew that talking was far more effective than shouting. This, from *The Weight of Glory*:

> It would seem that Our Lord finds our desires not too strong, but too weak. We are half-hearted creatures, fooling about with drink and sex and ambition when infinite joy is offered us, like an ignorant child who wants to go on making mud pies in a slum because he cannot imagine what is meant by the offer of a holiday at the sea. We are far too easily pleased.

And this, from *The Great Divorce*:

> There are only two kinds of people in the end: those who say to God, "Thy will be done," and those to whom God says, in the end, "Thy will be done." All that are in Hell, choose it. Without that self-choice there could be no Hell. No soul that seriously and constantly desires joy will ever miss it. Those who seek find. To those who knock it is opened.

In 1950, *The Lion, the Witch and the Wardrobe* was published, the first of seven books in the Narnia series. The Christian metaphors and imagery are obvious to most adults, but to children the stories are merely delicious and unforgettable. As such they have sown the seeds of belief in numerous young minds. The Christ-like figure of Aslan is introduced in the following passage:

"Aslan?" said Mr. Beaver. "Why, don't you know? He's the King. He's the Lord of the whole wood, but not often here, you understand. Never in my time or my father's time. But the word has reached us that he has come back. He is in Narnia at this moment. He'll settle the White Queen all right. It is he, not you, that will save Mr. Tumnus."

"Is – is he a man?" asked Lucy.

"Aslan a man!" Mr. Beaver said sternly. "Certainly not. I tell you he is the King of the wood and the son of the great Emperor-Beyond-the-Sea. Don't you know who is the King of Beasts? Aslan is a lion – *the* Lion, the great Lion."

"Ooh!" said Susan, "I'd thought he was a man. Is he – quite safe? I shall feel rather nervous about meeting a lion."

"That you will, dearie, and no mistake," said Mrs. Beaver; "if there's anyone who can appear before Aslan without their knees knocking, they're either braver than most or else just silly."[2]

In 1952, Lewis's *Mere Christianity* appeared. The title reflected the author's attempt to move Christianity away from those who would adapt it, alter it, dilute it, and change what is pure and pristine into something that is confused and confusing. He did not pepper his prose with quotes from the Scriptures because he knew that this would have a limited effect with the majority of his readers. What he did do was show that a belief in God was logical, and that from this belief an acceptance of Jesus Christ was unavoidable. He reversed the equation offered by the secular world, that it is the thoughtless who become Christians, the thoughtful who reject Christianity. Simply, he summed up the arguments like an angel:

> There is no need to be worried by facetious people who try to make the Christian hope of Heaven ridiculous by saying they do not want to spend eternity playing harps. The answer to such people is that if they cannot understand books written for grown-ups, they should not talk about them. All the scriptural imagery (harps, crowns, gold, etc.) is, of course, a merely symbolical attempt to express the inexpressible. People who take these symbols literally might as well think that when Christ told us to be like doves, He meant that we were to lay eggs.

This, from *Mere Christianity*:

Imagine yourself as a living house. God comes in to rebuild that house. At first, perhaps, you can understand what He is doing. He is getting the drains right and stopping the leaks in the roof and so on; you knew that those jobs needed doing and so you are not surprised. But presently He starts knocking the house about in a way that hurts abominably and does not seem to make any sense. What on earth is He up to? The explanation is that He is building quite a different house from the one you thought of – throwing out a new wing here, putting on an extra floor there, running up towers, making courtyards. You thought you were being made into a decent little cottage: but He is building a palace. He intends to come and live in it Himself.

In the 1950s Lewis met and fell in love with Joy Davidman, an American writer and convert from Judaism. The marriage was beautiful but brief, and Joy died in 1960. The movie *Shadowlands* chronicled some of the magnificence of the relationship but, sadly, managed to expunge most of the Christianity from the story. What brought them together, what sustained them during the agony of Joy's cancer, and what saved Lewis after the loss was a commitment to Jesus Christ. Just as in Lewis's day, the entertainment industry is not comfortable with such a notion. After Joy's death, Lewis wrote a short book titled *A Grief Observed*, an exploration of his own feelings following his wife's death. "Grief still feels like fear," he said. "Up till this time I always had too little time. Now there is nothing but time. Almost pure time, empty successiveness." He told friends he could no longer remember Joy's face. Until it came to him that she was there all along, just waiting. Her face shone again in his mind and God's love and certainty overwhelmed his pain.[3]

Though his remaining years were never as happy as those spent with Joy, Lewis wrote and lectured, becoming a famous man in Europe as well as North America. He died in 1963, on the same day as President Kennedy. Because of that his death received less coverage than it otherwise might have. Something that probably would have pleased Jack Lewis. Yet his funeral in Oxford was well attended, with so many people grieving. But grief was quite unnecessary. Lewis had known that what was to come was far greater than what we have already known. And he was reunited with Joy. As for the lion Aslan, some say they heard him roar all day, from Oxford to the ends of the Earth.

J.R.R. Tolkien was a contemporary, colleague, and friend of Lewis. Like Lewis, the author of *The Lord of the Rings* and *The Hobbit* was a devout and life-long Christian. But if Lewis had a loyal following, Tolkien is positively adored. So much so that when various bookstores, newspapers, magazines, and literary societies compiled their lists of all-time greats to mark the millennium, Tolkien won the contests over and over again. First it was a chain of stores, polling more than twenty-five thousand people. Charles Dickens, Leo Tolstoy, and Jane Austen did well, but the man with the pipe and tweeds, and friends in dwarfish places, came out on top. This annoyed the chattering classes and in particular the atheists no end, so the highly prestigious Folio Society asked its fifty thousand members what they thought. Connoisseurs of fine literature, these good men and women were certain to make a different choice. They didn't. The question was then taken to other countries, other languages, and changed into "Best Book of the Century," "Best Author of the Century," and even "Greatest Writer of the Millennium." Like it or not, Tolkien beat Joyce, Proust, and Balzac, prompting one British critic to say that this was why universal literacy and a publicly funded library system were not so desirable. He was joking. Just.

Because nothing is so unpopular with our elites as, yes, popularity. And Tolkien is as popular as they come. In the summer of 2000 the short trailer for *The Lord of the Rings* movies was put on the film company's official website as part of an early publicity blitz for the release of the first of the three productions. On the first day the trailer was available there were 1.5 million downloads, twice as many as the previous record, held by *Star Wars: The Phantom Menace*. Why? Or, in the words of those who hate the Oxford University professor with his tales of wizards, elves, battles and mystery, and Christian metaphor, why the hell does this awful man and his awful readers do so well? The support for Tolkien is fascinating, not only because of its size, but because of its diversity. Devotees of science fiction, fans of Dungeons and Dragons, Christians, zealots on the fringes of the political far right, dabblers in the occult, old hippies, and even the new wave of people opposed to globalization and free trade, are all drawn to the story.

The reason for the unholy alliance is really the nature of the man himself. He was a conservative Catholic, never happy with the reforms of the Second Vatican Council and somewhat sympathetic to the aspirations of Franco during the Spanish Civil War. This needs context. There were many British and North American Catholics who, while totally opposed to Hitler and Nazism, were shocked by the slaughter of priests and nuns by the Republicans in Spain and grudgingly preferred the Generalissimo to a left increasingly dominated by Stalinism and the Kremlin's thugs. Yet Tolkien was an anti-Nazi before it was altogether respectable, and indeed when many on the political left were still ambivalent. Shortly before the Second World War, a German publisher wrote to him and inquired about buying the rights to his works. They asked if he was an Aryan. He replied that the word made no linguistic or ethnic sense. But, he added, if they were in fact asking him if he had any Jewish blood he regretted that this was not the case, although he would like to have some connection with such a gifted people. He finished by telling the letter writer that he would never be allowed to publish him and that the Nazis were destroying German culture and the beauty of the northern spirit.[4]

Tolkien's religious conservatism simply did not transfer into political reaction. He viewed the industrialization of his beloved Warwickshire, that county in the middle of England that inspired the characters and locations in *The Lord of the Rings*, with unrestrained horror. The working people of his youth had, he thought, a spiritual and cultural autonomy, a special dignity. That had been expunged with the advance of the factory, the collective, and the multinational. As for globalization, Tolkien believed in the small community. He once said that Belgium was the perfect size for a country. Large enough to be distinct, small enough to feel like an extended family. The idea of universal free trade and a one-world corporate government terrified him. His fame and success was in essence an American phenomenon, or at least it began in the United States. Before American university students took up Tolkien's cause he had been successful on a much smaller scale. World famous in Oxford, so to speak. The new radicalism of the 1960s looked to a most surprising hero. Tolkien's books sold in quite staggering numbers and graffiti began to appear on college walls. Beneath slogans demanding withdrawal from Vietnam would be written, "Frodo Rules" and "Bilbo for President."

No surprise then that the man should be read again now by the pierced ranks determined to bring down Starbucks, Nike, and international capitalism. Science fiction and Dungeons and Dragons? The appeal is obvious. The issue here is that Tolkien initiated the whole thing. But whereas his emulators fill their books with babes in red leather leotards and muscular chaps in jerkins, Tolkien gave them character and depth and, yes, fundamentally Christian notions of value, virtue, and truth. So the fan base is a delicious mingling of types who would not normally give each other the time of day. But it must never be forgotten that everything Tolkien did, said, and wrote was informed by his Christianity. "All that is gold does not glitter, not all those who wander are lost; the old that is strong does not wither, deep roots are not reached by the frost," he writes in *The Lord of the Rings*. "From the ashes a fire shall be woken, a light from the shadows shall spring; renewed shall be blade that was broken, the crownless again shall be king." The meaning is obvious.[5]

The Christian beliefs of Dorothy L. Sayers, the British author who created the fictional detective Lord Peter Wimsey, were even more pronounced, because she wrote more often and more specifically about her faith. While the Wimsey stories are some of the most popular crime fiction books in the world, Sayers herself was far more proud of her Christianity and her Christian writing. She was born in Oxford in 1893. Her father was an Anglican vicar and chaplain of Christ Church College. She herself was educated at Oxford and was one of the first women to receive a full degree. After university, she worked as a writer in an advertising company and also began a relationship with an unemployed salesman named Bill White. The affair was sexual rather than loving, and Sayers became pregnant. White abandoned both mother and child when he heard the news and Sayers, anxious not to shock her aged parents, hid herself away and disguised her pregnancy. She told her employers that she was suffering from exhaustion and asked for an extended vacation. Young, alone, and frightened, she went to what was then known as a "mother's hospital," where in January 1924 John Anthony was born. She nursed him for three weeks and then arranged for the boy to be raised by her cousin. In 1926, Sayers fell in love with and married Atherton Fleming. They adopted John Anthony but, yielding to social pressures, Sayers never made it public that she was the boy's biological mother.[6]

Sayers began her writing career before both her marriage and her affair. As early as 1921 she wrote to a friend, "My detective story begins brightly, with a fat lady found dead in her bath with nothing on but her pince-nez. Now why did she wear pince-nez in her bath? If you can guess, you will be in a position to lay hands upon the murderer, but he's a very cool and cunning fellow. . . . " This was the foundation for the novel *Whose Body?*, published in 1923. It was the introduction of Lord Peter Wimsey to the world, and he was to entertain for ten books and two volumes of short stories. An aristocrat with a monocle, a pedigree, and an accent with which to cut the finest of glass, he was a decorated soldier, a gifted pianist, and, most of all, a consummate sleuth. With his faithful butler and helper he reappeared in *Clouds of Witness, Unnatural Death, The Unpleasantness at the Bellona Club,* and *Lord Peter Views the Body.* In 1930, Sayers published *Strong Poison,* the debut of Harriet Vane – she was also a detective novelist and, inevitably, the object of Wimsey's love. The fictional couple would marry, and in the 1937 *Busman's Honeymoon* set off on their eponymous honeymoon. Where they discover, as of course do so many newly married couples, a mysterious corpse. *The Nine Tailors, Gaudy Night, Five Red Herrings,* and *Have His Carcase,* among others, completed the Wimsey and Vane canon and they are still read by millions and televised on a regular basis.

The triumph of the Wimsey novels has often obscured the very real faith of their creator. It is Sayers the Christian whom we need to remember. Sayers always argued that her translation of Dante's *Divina Commedia* was her finest work, and she was also justifiably proud of her radio drama *The Man Born to Be King,* which C.S. Lewis re-read every Easter. Indeed, Sayers made some appearances at the Socratic Club in Oxford with Lewis, often to defend the Christian faith. Based on the life of Christ, the radio play is a cycle of twelve stories presenting various incidents in Scripture. It was originally broadcast on the BBC over a ten-month period and provoked opposition from atheist groups. It also led to opposition from some Christians who were offended by Jesus being depicted by any actor. Yet it was an enormous success and was turned into a book with accompanying notes from the author.

Sayers also wrote a pageant about the Emperor Constantine; a nativity play titled *He That Should Come*; a collection of essays, *Creed or Chaos*; and an extraordinary analysis of the Christian creative spirit called *The Mind of the Maker*. In 1943, the Archbishop of Canterbury offered her a special doctorate in divinity because of her contributions to Christian apologetics and literature. She declined. Seven years later, however, she did accept an honorary doctorate of letters from Durham University, an institution founded, perhaps ironically, by the seventeenth-century Puritan dictator Oliver Cromwell. He would not have approved of her rather high Anglicanism. Sayers was also concerned with the decline of Christian and classical education and her essay "The Lost Tools of Learning" is still used by many, especially in the home-schooling movement, as a structural guide to classical education. She died in December 1957, seven years after her husband.

In *Creed or Chaos? Why Christians Must Choose Either Dogma or Disaster*, Sayers wrote:

It is worse than useless for Christians to talk about the importance of Christian morality, unless they are prepared to take their stand upon the fundamentals of Christian theology. It is a lie to say that dogma does not matter; it matters enormously. It is fatal to let people suppose that Christianity is only a mode of feeling; it is vitally necessary to insist that it is first and foremost a rational explanation of the universe. It is hopeless to offer Christianity as a vaguely idealistic aspiration of a simple and consoling kind; it is, on the contrary, a hard, tough, exacting, and complex doctrine, steeped in a drastic and uncompromising realism. And it is fatal to imagine that everybody knows quite well what Christianity is and needs only a little encouragement to practice it. The brutal fact is that in this Christian country not one person in a hundred has the faintest notion what the Church teaches about God or man or society or the person of Jesus Christ. . . . Theologically this country is at present in a state of utter chaos established in the name of religious toleration and rapidly degenerating into flight from reason and the death of hope.

It's an approach and a belief that was echoed many times by Malcolm Muggeridge, and when the great writer and broadcaster died in 1990 it can be said without any fear of hyperbole that one of the most sparkling minds and souls of contemporary Christianity, literature, and the arts had passed on. His achievements were many and extraordinary: books such as *Jesus, The Man Who Lives*; *Paul, Envoy Extraordinary*; volumes of autobiography, biographies of Mother Teresa, delightfully clever and cutting accounts of twentieth-century history, and numerous television shows and radio appearances.

Malcolm Muggeridge was a satirist, a spy, and a raconteur, the author of legions of articles and essays and some of the wittiest and most penetrating television broadcasts we are ever likely to see. (Ironic, in that he claimed to despise television as a means of communication and would eventually boycott it.) He was perhaps the finest journalist of his age and could have demanded any job in British media. Instead, he chose to take up the cause of the unborn, the disabled, and Christian moral teaching. As a consequence he often found himself isolated and despised. A martyrdom, however, that as a dedicated follower of Christ he claimed that he always welcomed and embraced.

Born in south London, Muggeridge graduated from Cambridge University in 1924 and then taught in India, Egypt, and England before working as a journalist for the *Manchester Guardian*. In 1927, he married the writer and translator Kathleen Rosalind Dobbs, known as Kitty. She was the niece of the socialist author and activist Beatrice Webb. Along with so many other intellectuals of the era, they were attracted to Communism; unlike so many other intellectuals of the era they travelled to the Soviet Union and saw what a hellish social experiment in reality it had become. Muggeridge went to the Ukraine and witnessed the forced famine that was taking place. He smuggled back reports of this holocaust, but many of them were never printed and Soviet zealots and sympathizers in Europe and North America denied the accusations. Walter Duranty in the *New York Times* was particularly spiteful and dishonest and claimed that the Ukrainians were a healthy, wealthy people. He was joined by the likes of George Bernard Shaw and other socialist writers. It's significant that the massively influential *New York Times* went on to virtually ignore the attempted genocide of the Jewish people by Hitler. Muggeridge began to satirize the left in his writings, but never embraced a consistently right-wing position. His politics were too subtle for that. It was truth rather than power that fascinated the man.

During the Second World War, Muggeridge worked for the British Secret Intelligence Service, but abandoned espionage for journalism in the late 1940s. He worked for the *Evening*

Standard and the *Daily Telegraph* and then, in 1953, became editor of *Punch* magazine. *Punch* was an institution. Part serious columns, part humour, and renowned for its cartoons, it was a prestigious appointment. And Muggeridge was an outstanding editor. The magazine's later editor Alan Coren, my cousin, once explained that Muggeridge "imposed himself on the thing, made it even greater than it had been. And it had always been great." In the 1960s, Muggeridge became a regular broadcaster for the BBC and the personification of intelligent and ethical objection to the new permissiveness. On radio and television he would interview and comment, exposing the selfishness and sheer banality of so much of what was allegedly new and daring.[7]

It's no coincidence that the more Muggeridge saw of the waves of self-indulgence and sexual silliness in 1960s Western society, the more he swam toward the sea of faith. In 1967 he preached a famous sermon on his beliefs in Cambridge, and the following year he interviewed Mother Teresa. His documentary and book about her, *Something Beautiful for God*, presented the woman to the world. It was a perfect match. A literary giant and a tiny saint colliding in heavenly light. Millions watched the little Christian genius as she spread the love of Christ in the slums of Calcutta. Muggeridge was the conduit. He became public about his Christian faith, making short films about St. Augustine, William Blake, Pascal, Bonheoffer, and Kierkegaard. In 1982, he became a Roman Catholic. It was, he said, inevitable. There was only one institution that understood life and stood absolutely firm in its defence.

Since his death, Muggeridge has been quoted often in support and defence of Christianity, and quite right, too. This, for example, from *The End of Christendom*:

People think of faith as being something that you don't really believe, a device in helping you believe simply it. Of course that is quite wrong. As Pascal says, faith is a gift of God. It is different from the proof of it. It is the kind of faith God himself places in the heart, of which the proof is often the instrument. . . . He says of it, too, that it is the heart which is aware of God, and not reason. That is what faith is: God perceived by the heart, not by reason.

And this, when discussing Christianity's unique alternative to modern political and ideological excesses:

Against the new leviathan, whether in the guise of universal suffrage, democracy, or of an equally fraudulent triumphant proletariat, he (Kierkegaard) pitted the individual human soul made in the image of a God who was concerned about the fate of every living creature. In contrast with the notion of salvation through power, he held out the hope of salvation through suffering. The Cross against the ballot box or clenched fist; the solitary pilgrim against the slogan-shouting mob; the crucified Christ against the demagogue-dictators promising a kingdom of heaven on earth, whether achieved through endlessly expanding wealth and material well-being, or through the ever greater concentration of power and its ever more ruthless exercise.

Ah, if only he had been one of those clever atheists.

If Muggeridge was terrifyingly brilliant, Hilaire Belloc was brilliantly terrifying. He was born in 1870 in La Celle St. Cloud near Paris, during one of the fiercest and most relentless thunderstorms the area had ever seen; as a result he was known as "Old

Thunder" in his family. The sobriquet stayed with him because of his passion and style. Educated in England at the Oratory School in Birmingham and later at Balliol College Oxford, he became famous as a debater. Basil Joseph Mathews wrote a first-hand account of the young Belloc in argument:

> It was one of those rare nights in the Oxford Union when new men are discovered. Men whispered to each other of the future Gladstone and Dizzy whom Oxford was to give to the nation. No one would be fool enough to speak after such brilliant rhetoric. . . . Suddenly a young man rose and walked to the table. He was broad of shoulder and trod the floor confidently. A chin that was almost grim in its young strength was surmounted by a large squarely-built face. Over his forehead and absurdly experienced eyes, dark hair fell stiffly. As he rose, men started up and began to leave the house; at his first sentence they paused and looked at him – and sat down again. By the end of his third sentence, with a few waves of his powerful hands, and a touch of unconscious magnetism and conscious strength, Mr. Hilaire Belloc held his audience breathless.

Author and Christian activist Gregory McDonald knew Belloc and described him as "the most ruthless, effective and unforgiving writer of polemic, and sustainer of argument and debate, whom I have ever encountered. He was a combination of bulldog and bloodhound: once he got his teeth into you, he never let go; and once he had your scent, he never gave up." Anecdotes about his rude behaviour are legion, as are stories of his verbal skill. His friend and biographer J.B. Morton, however, wrote in more defensive terms: "The point I would make is that Belloc dominated not by insensitive loudness, but by the force of his character. He talked with authority, and his presence suggested authority." He wrote 156 books and pamphlets during his long and opinionated career, was elected as a Member of Parliament, served in the French artillery, and spearheaded, with G.K. Chesterton, Catholic letters and literature for almost half a century. He was a poet, a novelist, an essayist, a historian, and an editor. *The Bad Child's Book of Beasts* was published in 1896, then *The Path to Rome*, and *The Party System* – the latter written with G.K. Chesterton's brother Cecil. The following years saw *The Servile State*, *Europe and the Faith*, and *Belinda*. There were also biographies of Oliver Cromwell, James II, Napoleon, and various other historically significant figures, books on the Crusades, the Reformation, and the history of his Church.[8]

This is important. The Church. The central feature of the man's life and work was not a defence of country or party or person but of the Christian Church. Indeed he despised parties and the party system and realized that much of the parliamentary game was a sham and a digression from the deeper issues. In this, as with so many aspects of public life, Belloc was acutely perceptive and predictive. His books on Islam, for example, speak of the clash of civilizations that would transform Europe, generations before the onset of mass Muslim immigration into the West. He was not always humble, but he was invariably correct. He saw the threat of eugenics and of abortion; he was sharp and clear about the coming modernist attack on concepts of right and wrong and the rape of the culture by moral relativism. He wrote of these monsters long before any other author of note did so. He wrote and he warned.

We sit by and watch the Barbarian, we tolerate him; in the long stretches of peace we are not afraid. We are tickled by his irreverence, his comic inversion of our old certitudes and our fixed creeds refreshes us; we laugh. But as we laugh we are watched by large and awful faces from beyond: and on those faces there is no smile.

Belloc died in 1953, an isolated and somewhat neglected figure. It is no mere coincidence that the renewal of interest in the man comes as we face ceaseless attacks upon his beloved Christianity.

If there is a renewed interest in Belloc, there is an entire industry surrounding his friend G.K. Chesterton. We are generally not well served by journalism today, and Christian journalists in particular sometimes seem more intent on pleasing their secular friends than in defending the Christian Church. Oh, for another Gilbert Keith Chesterton, who wrote the truth of permanent things, of first things, of Christian things. Born in 1874 in London, England, he enjoyed the best in British private education, but chose not to go to university, which partly explains his visceral refusal to adopt convention and think and write within partisan definitions. He drifted into journalism, but once afloat he sailed perfectly, and often against the wind. On the fashionable nationalism of the Edwardian age, for example: "My country, right or wrong, is a thing that no patriot would think of saying except in a desperate case. It is like saying, my mother, drunk or sober." On literature: "A good novel tells us the truth about its hero; but a bad novel tells us the truth about its author." On being controversial: "I believe in getting into hot water, it keeps you clean." Books came early and frequently. *Greybeards at Play* in 1900, *Twelve Types* in 1902, a biography of Robert Browning the following year. Then in 1904 one of his finest works, *The Napoleon of Notting Hill*. Ostensibly about a London district declaring independence from Great Britain, at heart it explained Chesterton's belief that the state was more often a problem than a solution, and the greater the intervention of government the more profound the damage to the governed.

Chesterton married Frances Blogg in 1901, and they had an intensely happy, though childless, life together. She was a steadying influence on his notorious untidiness and lack of organization. "Am at Market Harborough," he once wrote to her. "Where ought I to be?" Her reply? "Home." At a time when H.G. Wells was celebrating infidelity and George Bernard Shaw was deconstructing marriage, Chesterton insisted that family was at the centre of any civilized society. In 1922, he became a Roman Catholic. "The fight for the family and the free citizen and everything decent must now be waged by the one fighting form of Christianity," he wrote. And, "The Christian ideal has not been tried and found wanting; it has been found difficult and left untried."

Step forward the grand knight of the Christian faith. With his brother Cecil and with Hilaire Belloc, he embraced Distributism, based on concepts of family autonomy and small-scale production leading to authentic democracy. Neither socialist nor capitalist, and never liberal in the contemporary sense. "A citizen can hardly distinguish between a tax and a fine, except that the fine is generally much lighter," and "Too much capitalism does not mean too many capitalists, but too few capitalists." He possessed a sparkling ability to hold up a mirror to the addled society around him and show its absurd reflection. "Journalism largely consists of saying 'Lord Jones is dead' to people who never knew that Lord Jones was alive." And, "The Bible tells us to love our neighbours, and also to love our enemies; probably because they are generally the same people."[9]

There were biographies of St. Francis, St. Thomas Aquinas, and Charles Dickens, compilations of columns and journalism, an autobiography, and works of apologetics and history such as *Orthodoxy*, *Heretics*, and *The Everlasting Man*. There was also poetry – *The Ballad of the White Horse* and *Lepanto* – and the creation of the priest-detective Father Brown. Chesterton was as witty as Oscar Wilde, as original as James Joyce, as clever as Franz Kafka, yet he remains an icon to too few, partly because he spoke and wrote as a Christian. In the final years of his life, Chesterton predicted that the absolutes of right and wrong would become blurred, religion publicly condemned, and that we would care more for animals than babies, and would worship sex while mocking love. We would, he said, be governed by whim and fashion.

Tradition means giving votes to the most obscure of all classes, our ancestors. It is the democracy of the dead. Tradition refuses to submit to that arrogant oligarchy who merely happen to be walking around.

He was, quite clearly, not only a fine writer but also a prophet, and a prophet who wrote beautifully and lyrically about his faith:

You say grace before meals. All right. But I say grace before the concert and the opera, and grace before the play and pantomime, and grace before I open a book, and grace before sketching, painting, swimming, fencing, boxing, walking, playing, dancing and grace before I dip the pen in the ink.

Or, in his seminal book *Orthodoxy*,

According to most philosophers, God in making the world enslaved it. According to Christianity, in making it, He set it free. God had written, not so much a poem, but rather a play; a play he had planned as perfect, but which had necessarily been left to human actors and stage-managers, who had since made a great mess of it.

Evelyn Waugh was also a convert to Christianity, but not as active an apologist for the faith as Chesterton. Nevertheless, he was a dedicated Christian from his conversion until his death, and also one of the finest novelists of the twentieth century. Born in 1903, Waugh was the author of, among others, *Brideshead Revisited, Decline and Fall, Scoop, A Handful of Dust, Vile Bodies, Black Mischief, Put Out More Flags,* and biographies of Ronald Knox and Edmund Campion. He was also a man who recorded and predicted moral decay and the culture of death with more skill, humour, and foresight than any of his literary contemporaries.

He was born into a wealthy if not prestigious middle-class family and educated privately and at Oxford University. He did little work, and when asked in an interview what he did for his college he replied, "I drank for it." He became a teacher after university, but a reluctant and cynical one. He had always written, and in 1928 after dabbling in journalism, he published *Decline and Fall,* a biting satire about social climbing, the upper classes, and the fortune and misfortune of an innocent young teacher. Two years later came *Vile Bodies,* a hilarious account of bright young things and their dark old sins, establishing Waugh as one of Britain's foremost young writers. In the same year he became a Roman Catholic. Some years later, when he was behaving badly at a fashionable dinner party he was asked how he could be so rude and still call himself a Christian. "Imagine how insufferable I would be," he replied, "if I were not!"

Brideshead Revisited was published in 1945 and was Waugh's most forthright exploration of his faith. His characters are the personification of charm and style and grace, but the author shows us the spiritual longings behind the obvious glamour. Once again, there is a theme of decline, replicated in his *Sword of Honour* trilogy, published between 1952 and 1961. The books are based on Waugh's own wartime service in an elite combat unit and chronicle the disillusionment of its hero, who saw at first hand the moral and political corruption of all man-made ideology. Waugh was one of the few writers of the era willing to condemn Communism, in this case that of the Yugoslavian partisans. The final book of the three shows the quintessential inhumanity of collectivism and how a society without Godly absolutes is destined to destroy itself and, unless stopped, those around it. Waugh's *Life of Monsignor Ronald Knox*, one of the finest minds of his generation, was a tender study of a great friend and a great Christian. As with his biography of Elizabethan saint Edmund Campion, it is relatively uncritical but relentlessly reliable and moving.[10]

Waugh died in 1966 after returning home from church on Easter Sunday, with his wife and children in the next room. Almost fifty years later, his writing is more popular than ever. But it his approach to the world's squabbles and quarrels rather than his specific work that is so timeless. He saw his Christian faith as being the only rock of sanity in a sea of modernist screaming and hateful philosophies. Critics have argued that he retreated from the world; the truth is that he advanced into faith.

And his comments and observations are as penetrating and accurate today as when they were written. "Pray always for all the learned, the oblique, the delicate. Let them not be quite forgotten at the throne of God when the simple come into their kingdom" and "There is a species of person called a 'Modern Churchman' who draws the full salary of a beneficed clergyman and need not commit himself to any religious belief." This, of course, was more than half a century before the liberal lunacies of the modern Christianity we now know so well. Or, on the glorious simplicity of sainthood, "Saints are simply men and women who have fulfilled their natural obligation which is to approach God."

This is just a sampling of intellectually gifted Christian authors, all of them from the modern era. If we went back in history the list would fill a far longer book than this. If we went beyond literature to other areas of arts and culture, the book would become a library. In its earliest days, the Christian religion was mocked in the cities and by the elites as being the faith of slaves and peasants, of the foolish and rural people. It's fascinating, and not without significance, that two thousand years later something similar has developed. The Christians are the ones who do not think, who do not read, and are not sophisticated. This notion is as wrong now as ever it was then.

HITLER WAS A CHRISTIAN

THERE IS NO BETTER WAY of winning an argument than to accuse an opponent of being a Nazi or a fascist. When it comes to accusing Christianity of being horribly right-wing and reactionary, why not go straight to the heart of hatred and talk about the Nazis? What is the definition of a racist? Someone who is winning an argument against an atheist. In fact the National Socialists were so evil, and their regime and the Holocaust it produced so repugnant, that we should only use the word Nazi when we are speaking specifically of Nazis and Nazism. Today, however, it is used in particular by the left to condemn conservatives, and increasingly by opponents of Israel to demonize the Jewish state in a sickening display of dark paradox. So the word Nazi tends to end an argument, close a debate, put a stop to intelligent discussion. Equally, to claim that Adolf Hitler was a Christian and that Nazism was sympathetic to Christianity or even a product of it, and that Christianity supported Nazism, is a clumsy but surprisingly successful way to discredit Christians and Christianity. Of course, logically even if it was true, it would be irrelevant. Bad people can claim to be good, bad ideas can hide behind good ones, and so on. Evil has been committed in the name of Christianity, just as it has in the name of non-Christianity or anti-Christianity. Evil is committed in the name of pretty much everything. It demonstrates the fallen nature of humanity, and precisely why we need Christ. But was Hitler a Christian, and did Nazism grow as a natural consequence out of Christianity, and was it supported by Christian leaders?

Despite the number of times that this is alleged, the answer is still *no*. Pure and simple. *No, no, no.* Part of the problem is geographical. Nazism developed in Europe, and while German armies and Nazi ideology spread beyond the European continent, it was at heart a European phenomenon. As Europe had been the heartland of Christianity since the early medieval period, it should come as no surprise that most of the followers of National Socialism had been born into Christian families and raised in a nominally Christian environment. As, of course, had the British, American, Canadian, Australian, French, Polish, Russian, and various other people who fought against the Nazis and were their victims. But history and fact require more than geopolitical accident or historical incident. Basic questions, free of the infection of prejudgement, need to be asked. Nazism is more than the Hollywood caricature of angry men with bad accents and worse moustaches, and to think of the National Socialist German Workers Party as being composed purely of brutes and Neanderthals is to fail to grasp the more profound malice of the movement. This was a party and a spasm with an ideology, and when the toxins of racism were injected into the bloodstream of the German body politic, it was not an infection that had Christian origins. Various right-wing organizations had existed throughout Europe for some time, with varying degrees of attachment to a monarchy, a particular period of perceived historical national glory, an all-powerful state, an aggressive foreign policy, or some blurred and often confused form of racial purity system. Some of them supported the Christian Church, because they saw faith and church as a bulwark of tradition, continuity, and stability. Sometimes, in certain areas, some members of these churches reciprocated, assuming the political right would be a defence against Marxism and socialism, creeds that often attacked the Church, destroyed churches, and killed and persecuted Christians, as soon as they came to power. To an extent, then, reaction was understandable. There were also, however, Christians and churches that openly opposed the far right and even supported the left.

Nazism was something entirely different. It took its inspiration from the left as well as the right and always regarded itself as being anti-capitalist as well as anti-Marxist. Indeed it was, according to its adherents, a third way: it claimed to be the great truth that existed between Slavonic, Jewish bolshevism on the one hand, and Anglo-Saxon, Jewish capitalism on the other. In the drunken imagination of the Nazis, the Jews magically managed to lead both sides of the great enemy. And it was the Jewish people who gave us Jesus, gave us His mother Mary, gave us His stepfather Joseph, gave us St. Peter, St. Paul, most of the writers of the New Testament, most of the early martyrs of the Church. It was the Jews about whom was written the Old Testament, which represents the literary and theological origins of the Christian faith. This Jewish context was why the French enlightenment philosopher Voltaire, for example, was so anti-Semitic. He hated Christianity and blamed the Jews for giving the world Christ. Judaism, he wrote, "dares spread an irreconcilable hatred against all nations; it revolts against all its masters. Always superstitious, always avid of the well-being enjoyed by others, always barbarous, crawling in misfortune, and insolent in prosperity." While Voltaire detested Christianity and thus Judaism for, in his eyes, encouraging superstition and of course religion, the Nazis hated Christianity and thus Judaism, for encouraging weakness and charity, and destroying the Germanic, pagan ideal of strength, aggression, and the apotheosis of the human soul and spirit through war, blood, and conquest. At the periphery of Nazism there were numerous hazy, reactionary ideas, but at the core of the movement and its ideology was a profound, vehemently anti-Christian belief in the new man, free of the shackles of the teachings of the Jew Jesus.[1]

Hitler himself stated in July 1941:

National Socialism and religion cannot exist together . . . . The heaviest blow that ever struck humanity was the coming of Christianity. Bolshevism is Christianity's illegitimate child. Both are inventions of the Jew. The deliberate lie in the matter of religion was introduced into the world by Christianity . . . . Let it not be said that Christianity brought man the life of the soul, for that evolution was in the natural order of things.

Four months later, he remarked:

Christianity is a rebellion against natural law, a protest against nature. Taken to its logical extreme, Christianity would mean the systematic cultivation of the human failure. . . .

and

The best thing is to let Christianity die a natural death . . . . When understanding of the universe has become widespread . . . Christian doctrine will be convicted of absurdity . . . . Christianity has reached the peak of absurdity . . . . And that's why someday its structure will collapse . . . . The only way to get rid of Christianity is to allow it to die little by little . . . .

Christianity the liar . . . . We'll see to it that the Churches cannot spread abroad teachings in conflict with the interests of the State.

Hardly pro-Christian stuff. It might sound deranged, but it's not dramatically different from what we hear from many atheists today, often the very people who tell us that Hitler was a Christian.

The former Austrian corporal continued,

The reason why the ancient world was so pure, light and serene was that it knew nothing of the two great scourges: the pox and Christianity,

and

Originally, Christianity was merely an incarnation of Bolshevism, the destroyer . . . . The decisive falsification of Jesus' doctrine was the work of St. Paul. He gave himself to this work . . . for the purposes of personal exploitation . . . . Didn't the world see, carried on right into the Middle Ages, the same old system of martyrs, tortures, faggots? Of old, it was in the name of Christianity. Today, it's in the name of Bolshevism. Yesterday the instigator was Saul: the instigator today, Mardochai. Saul was changed into Paul, and Mardochai into Karl Marx. By exterminating this pest, we shall do humanity a service of which our soldiers can have no idea.

Nor was this an occasional rant, provoked by some alleged Christian resistance, or just the wanderings and wonderings of a man who was always giving his opinions about religion and faith. Hitler was actually quite guarded in private, and while he certainly gave his views on Jews and Communists, it is stunning how often in these relatively few outbursts he attacks Christianity. In fact, there were several occasions when his rants about Christians were more severe and more common than his venom against Jews.

> Christianity is an invention of sick brains: one could imagine nothing more senseless, nor any more indecent way of turning the idea of the Godhead into a mockery . . . . When all is said, we have no reason to wish that the Italians and Spaniards should free themselves from the drug of Christianity. Let's be the only people who are immunised against the disease.

Speaking of fellow Nazi Hanns Kerrl, who from July 1935 was Reichsminister of Church Affairs, Hitler stated that the man,

> with noblest of intentions, wanted to attempt a synthesis between National Socialism and Christianity. I don't believe the thing's possible, and I see the obstacle in Christianity itself . . . . Pure Christianity – the Christianity of the catacombs – is concerned with translating Christian doctrine into facts. It leads quite simply to the annihilation of mankind. It is merely whole-hearted Bolshevism, under a tinsel of metaphysics.[2]

The following year, 1942, Hitler told his colleagues:

> It would always be disagreeable for me to go down to posterity as a man who made concessions in this field. I realize that man, in his imperfection, can commit innumerable

errors – but to devote myself deliberately to errors, that is something I cannot do. I shall never come personally to terms with the Christian lie. Our epoch in the next 200 years will certainly see the end of the disease of Christianity . . . . My regret will have been that I couldn't . . . behold.

It's quite obviously true that Hitler and some of the other Nazi leaders sometimes paid lip service to Christianity, and occasionally tried to placate Christian opposition, and even seduce Christians or nominal Christians into the Nazi ranks, but the idea that we should suddenly believe what the Nazis said in public when they were trying to win support is frankly ludicrous. They were killers, they were torturers, they were liars. Their public utterances, made for reasons of political expediency, simply cannot be trusted. In *Mein Kampf* itself, that laborious autobiographical handbook of evil, Hitler explained that propaganda

must be addressed always and exclusively to the masses. . . . The function of propaganda does not lie in the scientific training of the individual, but in calling the masses' attention to certain facts, processes, necessities, etc., whose significance is thus for the first time placed within their field of vision. The whole art consists in doing this so skilfully that everyone will be convinced that the fact is real, the process necessary, the necessity correct, etc. But since propaganda is not and cannot be the necessity in itself . . . its effect for the most part must be aimed at the emotions and only to a very limited degree at the so-called intellect. . . . Its soundness is to be measured exclusively by its effective result.

To prove his point, just a few months before the outbreak of the Second World War, Hitler told an eager audience that

amongst the accusations which are directed against Germany in the so called democracies is the charge that the National Socialist State is hostile to religion. In answer to that charge I should like to make before the German people the following solemn declaration: No one in Germany has in the past been persecuted because of his religious views, nor will anyone in the future be so persecuted.

It is an overwhelmingly fatuous and intellectually insulting comment, and with hindsight any rational person would dismiss this claim as the boast of a hugely immoral, unbalanced man intent on world power, never allowing truth and scruples to stand in his way. But this very statement has been used repeatedly to support the argument that Hitler was a friend of the Christian Church. This is Internet scholarship, and mere soundbite argument.[3]

If Hitler was a friend of any religious creed, it was paganism; unlike Christianity, the fantasy of paganism is extremely popular today. While Hitler and some of his colleagues made overtures to the more gullible and credulous of Christians, the heart of Nazism was not only anti-Christian because the Jews gave the world Christ, but because fascism in its northern European form looked to an atavistic past, an imaginary pure dawn before the advent of Christianity. Put simply, Nazism as a creed was inherently pagan, and while many of its supporters were mere thugs without any thought for religion, its most ardent ideological followers were pagan devotees. We see this in the German Faith Movement, which was conceived as an alternative to Christianity, and had its followers parade under the banner of the golden sun-wheel, sing the "Song of the Goths" as they marched, and celebrate pagan festivals. While the Faith Movement was never the mass organization its founders hoped it would be, it had the personal support of leading Nazis, who applauded its attempt to replace "Jew-riddled Christianity" with a "pure" Teutonic theology. Similarly, the Hitler Youth Movement – membership in which became compulsory once the Nazis came to power – indoctrinated young boys into pagan thought and ritual, and emphasized the anti-German and anti-Hitlerian nature of Christianity. The Nazi government also banned all Catholic and Protestant youth movements, because they were frightened that these Christian bodies would teach anti-Nazi ideas and diminish the influence of Nazism over young people. Again, hardly an indication of a warm relationship between Hitler and Christianity. One of the Hitler Youth organization's favourite and most popular marching songs contained the following words:

> We follow not Christ, but Horst Wessel,
> Away with incense and Holy Water,
> The Church can go hang for all we care,
> The Swastika brings salvation on Earth.

Horst Wessel had been killed by Communists earlier in the Nazi party's history, and though he had been an uncouth bully with few redeeming features, he was transformed into a Nazi hero and considered a martyr. Consider the contrast between the gentle, forgiving martyrs of Christianity, and the storm-trooping madmen who died for National Socialism.[4]

It is worth spending a little more time on the essentially pagan ethos at the root of Nazism, particularly as many of the most aggressive of modern anti-Christians have some sympathy if not downright passion for ideas such as pantheism, native spirituality, and anything they see as New Age or pre-Christian and an alternative to the Christian faith. That much of this flummery is modern, contrived, and the product more of Hollywood frolics than ancient forests seems to escape them. If Hitler was an anti-Christian and dreamed of a world without Christ and Christianity, his lieutenant and the head of the SS, Heinrich Himmler, was a devoted and obsessive pagan who intended to transform the SS into a "pure" pagan imperial force, where northern gods such as Odin were worshipped, where Christian concepts of family and community were expunged, and where women were used merely as a vehicle for producing more members of the pristine Aryan race: there was also a cult of homosexuality within the SS, where men were encouraged to use women to procreate, but were encouraged to replicate the Greek, Hellenistic ideal of love of male warrior for male warrior. Once again, because of the Christian defence of natural law and of sex being acceptable only within marriage between a man and a woman, this often put the churches into direct conflict with ideological Nazism. It's an area seldom mentioned today, partly because of the understandable sensitivity surrounding the persecution of gay men – lesbians were not acknowledged by the Nazis – during the Holocaust, but also because of a politically correct cloak of censorship that often makes honest and open conversation difficult if not impossible. The place of homosexuals in modern history demands an informed courtesy, but from all sides.

Some of the songs of the Nazi party also reveal a great deal of the mass, popular sentiment around the issue of religion, and that sentiment is bitingly anti-Christian. This song was particularly popular in Baden, and there is direct reference to it as early as 1935:

> Pope and rabbi shall yield,
> We want to be pagans again.
> No longer creep into the churches.
> The orb of the sun alone is leading us.
> Out with the Jews,
> And with the pope from the German home.

Another song, from the year before:

> We are the happy Hitler Youth,
> We need no Christian virtues,
> For our Fuhrer Adolf Hitler
> Is always our mediator.
> No parson, no evil man can prevent us
> From feeling ourselves to be Hitler children,
> We do not follow Christ but Horst Wessel,
> Away with incense and holy water vessels.
> We follow our flags singing,
> As worthy sons of our ancestors,
> I am no Christian, no Catholic,
> I go with the SA through thick and thin.
> I can do without the Church,
> The Swastika is redemption on earth. . . .

President Franklin D. Roosevelt was fed reports of the Nazis' anti-Christian activity by staff at his embassy and by various friendly diplomats before Hitler took power, right up until Germany declared war on the U.S. in December 1941. The U.S.

president had no illusions about Nazism's relationship with organized religion and in particular with the Christian faith, and wrote:

> It is a plan to abolish all existing religions, Catholic, Protestant, Mohammedan, Hindu, Buddhist, and Jewish alike. . . . The cross and all other symbols of religion are to be forbidden. The clergy are to be ever liquidated, silenced under penalty of the concentration camps, where even now so many fearless men are being tortured because they have placed God above Hitler. In the place of the churches of our civilization there is to be set up an international Nazi church, a church which will be served by orators sent out by the Nazi government. And in the place of the Bible, the words of "Mein Kampf" will be imposed and enforced as Holy Writ. And in the place of the cross of Christ will be put two symbols, the swastika and the naked sword.[5]

In January 1942, the *New York Times*, certainly not now and not really even then a particular friend of Christianity, published a thirty-point program listing the central dogmas of the National Reich Church, a body established by the Nazis to replace Christianity and to eliminate Christian ideas from the next generation of young Germans. It's significant that the *Times* published this, because if such an internationally important newspaper was aware of Nazism's hatred of Christianity, we can be sure it was a known and accepted fact elsewhere. Of the full thirty points, some are particularly significant. The list begins with this:

> The National Reich Church specifically demands the immediate turning over to its possession of all churches and chapels, to become national churches.

Then,

The National Reich Church is immutably fixed in its one objective: to destroy that Christian belief imported into Germany in the unfortunate year 800, whose tenets conflict with both the heart and mentality of the German.

It continues:

The National Reich Church demands the immediate cessation of the printing of the Bible, as well as its dissemination, throughout the Reich and colonies. All Sunday papers with any religious content shall also be suppressed,

and

The National Reich Church shall see that the importation of the Bible and other religious works into Reich territory is made impossible.

Point 15:

The National Reich Church decrees that the most important document of all time – therefore the guiding document of the German people – is the book of our Fuhrer, *Mein Kampf*. It recognizes that this book contains the principles of the purist ethnic morals under which the German people must live,

and then,

The National Reich Church will see to it that this book spreads its active forces among the entire population and that all Germans live by it,

and

The National Reich Church will remove from the altars of all churches the Bible, the cross and religious objects. . . . In their places will be set that which must be venerated by the German people and therefore is by God, our most saintly book, *Mein Kampf*, and to the left of this a sword.

Point 21:

In the National Reich Church there will be no remission of sins; its tenet is that, once committed, a sin is irrevocable and will be implacably punished by the laws of nature and in this world.

And finally,

On the day of the foundation of the National Reich Church the Christian cross shall be removed from all churches, cathedrals, and chapels inside the frontiers of the Reich and its colonies and will be replaced by the symbol of invincible Germany – the swastika.

Nor was this anti-Christian fetish unknown to contemporaries, from the most senior positions to the relatively junior, and in particular inside Germany itself. The case of the former Waffen SS officer Gereon Goldmann, for example, is fascinating.

Born in 1916, he was a Catholic who as a young man joined a Jesuit youth organization and had numerous street fights with teenage Nazis. At the age of nineteen, he entered a Franciscan seminary, but he was then drafted into the German Army and was transferred to the Waffen SS and based in Poland. He witnessed horrible atrocities, of course, and as a Christian did all he could to stop the barbarism. He was soon arrested as an anti-Nazi and sentenced to execution, only avoiding death when he was transferred instead to the eastern front. He wrote of the appalling treatment given to other German soldiers who were Christian and who as a consequence rejected Nazism and would not participate in any brutality. They were loyal Germans, willing to fight for their country, but as Christians were seen as not being true patriots or able to fit into the new Germany. Goldmann wrote:

> One day a big shot from Berlin came to speak to us.
>
> We were stunned by what he said, but we weren't allowed to tell anyone – it was strictly confidential. This man told us that "Victory could only be complete when all the churches were destroyed. Not only the Jewish religion, but also all Christian faiths would have to be eliminated."

Even the very position of Hitler as Fuhrer is directly contradictory to Christian beliefs. This role was not akin to that of prime minister, chancellor, or even president or king, but implied something Messianic and god-like. In fact there were many Nazis who saw Hitler as being if not the Son of God, a Christ-like figure sent directly by God to save the chosen people, the Germans. Hitler agreed: "How lucky I am that providence sent me to the desperate German people as a saviour in their hour of need." So he was more than a dictator, more than a skilled politician and orator who had managed to gain power through propaganda, a smashed world economy, military humiliation, and a flawed electoral system; he was a god. Ernest Jackh, the author of *The War for Man's Soul*, described the German population's attitude toward their leader:

> In its mind the mass sublimates the Fuhrer into a mystical phenomenon. It hails him as a "nationalistic Godsend" or as God himself and does not realize that nationalistic narrowness and God can never meet on the same plane. Similarly it elevates the physical importance of its leader into the realm of the superhuman, where there is no place for sensual human impulses and worships it as "sacred celibacy."

A German soldier dying in France told a French man who offered him some comfort in his final moments,

> The Fuhrer is my faith. I don't want anything from your church. But if you want to be good to me, get my Fuhrer's picture out of my pocket . . . My Fuhrer, I am happy to die for you!

Beyond the argument that Hitler was a Christian, and that he was supported and formed by Christians, is the scurrilous accusation we hear repeatedly that the Roman Catholic Church and its leader, Pope Pius XII, supported fascism and Nazism. What surprises many people is how recent this charge is. For two decades following the end of the Second World War and the revelations about the horrors of the Holocaust, the Catholic Church was understood to have been a central part of the anti-Nazi alliance. This was not doubted, and the positive image of the Church during the war was so overwhelming that the World Jewish Congress donated a great deal of money to the Vatican, largely in gratitude for what it had done to save Jewish lives. In 1945, Rabbi Herzog of Jerusalem, one of the most significant figures in the international Jewish community, thanked Pope Pius "for his lifesaving efforts on behalf of the Jews during the occupation of Italy." He continued,

The people of Israel will never forget what His Holiness and his illustrious delegates, inspired by the eternal principles of religion, which form the very foundation of true civilization, are doing for our unfortunate brothers and sisters in the most tragic hour of our history, which is living proof of Divine Providence in this world.

When the Pope died in 1958, Golda Meir, then Israeli foreign minister, later prime minister and a national hero and symbol in her country, delivered a eulogy at the United Nations, praising the man for his work on behalf of her people:

We share in the grief of humanity (at the death of Pius XII). When fearful martyrdom came to our people in the decade of Nazi terror, the voice of the pope was raised for the victims. The life of our times was enriched by a voice speaking out on the great moral truths above the tumult of daily conflict. We mourn a great servant of peace.

Rabbi Louis Finkelstein, chancellor of the Jewish Theological Seminary of America, wrote, "No keener rebuke has come to Nazism than from Pope Pius XI and his successor,

Pope Pius XII," and Rabbi Alexander Safran, the chief rabbi of Romania, stated:

> In the most difficult hours of which we Jews of Romania have passed through, the generous assistance of the Holy See . . . was decisive and salutary. It is not easy for us to find the right words to express the warmth and consolation we experienced because of the concern of the supreme pontiff, who offered a large sum to relieve the sufferings of deported Jews . . . . The Jews of Romania will never forget these facts of historic importance.

Nor did this enthusiasm come only from Jewish organizations and leaders. In 1941, after the Pope's Christmas address, the *Times* wrote:

> The voice of Pius XII is a lonely voice in the silence and darkness enveloping Europe this Christmas. . . . In calling for a "real new order" based on "liberty, justice and love" . . . the pope put himself squarely against Hitlerism.

Moshe Sharett would become Israel's first foreign minister and later second prime minister. He said,

> I told [Pope Pius XII] that my first duty was to thank him, and through him the Catholic Church, on behalf of the Jewish public for all they had done in the various countries to rescue Jews . . . . We are deeply grateful to the Catholic Church.

Albert Einstein, one of the most famous Jewish figures in world history and a man who was offered the presidency of Israel, said,

Only the Catholic Church protested against the Hitlerian onslaught on liberty. Up till then I had not been interested in the Church, but today I feel a great admiration for the Church, which alone has had the courage to struggle for spiritual truth and moral liberty.

Another Jewish man was closer to the relevant events than almost anyone. In 1945, the Chief Rabbi of Rome, Israel Zolli, publicly embraced Roman Catholicism, taking the baptismal name of Eugenio in honour of the Pope. This extraordinary and controversial conversion was partly due to Zolli's admiration for the Pope's sheltering and saving of Italian Jews.[6]

The general attitude began to change in the mid-1960s, largely after the 1963 publication of German writer Rolf Hochhuth's play *The Deputy*. Hochhuth is an unlikely witness and expert, in that he was an obsessive anti-Christian and would in his later years defend the infamous British Holocaust-denier David Irving. But the 1960s were an opportune time, with a hunger for anything that questioned authority and religion. In spite of being singularly uninspiring and long-winded, the play had an enormous influence with its accusations that Pope Pius XII was frightened of speaking out against the Nazis and was even supportive of their anti-Semitism. Hochhuth knew that the Pope had been deeply opposed to Nazi racism, because he admitted this privately to friends, but the *canard* was too good to destroy. In fact, the Catholic Church's opposition to Adolf Hitler and Nazism began long before 1939 or the beginnings of the Holocaust. On April 28, 1935, Eugenio Maria Giuseppe Giovanni Pacelli, later Pope Pius XII, spoke to more than a quarter of a million people in Lourdes, France. These were pilgrims from all over the world, and the intention was that they would take any message they heard from a papal representative back to their home countries. Pacelli told them that the German Nazis

> are in reality only miserable plagiarists who dress up old errors with new tinsel. It does not make any difference whether they flock to the banners of social revolution, whether they are guided by a false concept of the world and of life, or whether they are possessed by the superstition of a race and blood cult.

What is notable about this speech is that it wasn't notable. Pacelli had made other such speeches in public, and in private meetings had repeatedly expressed his opposition to Nazism and concerns about the rise of racism. The Berlin regime was well aware of this and considered Pacelli as problematic as even the Pope, Pius XI, who in 1937 wrote an entire papal encyclical, *Mit Brennender Sorge*, outlining the dangers and horrors of Nazi ideology. The following year, Pacelli told a group of Belgian pilgrims that "it is impossible for a Christian to take part in anti-Semitism. Anti-Semitism is inadmissible; spiritually, we are all Semites."

The general attitude within European diplomatic circles was that the Vatican's hostility toward Nazism was too extreme, and Catholic officials often found themselves questioned by secular representatives who, while opposed to Nazism, thought that the times required a gentler, more conciliatory approach. Dr. Joseph Lichten was a Polish Jewish diplomat who would later work for the Anti-Defamation League of B'nai Brith. He wrote,

> Pacelli had obviously established his position clearly, for the Fascist governments of both Italy and Germany spoke out

vigorously against the possibility of his election to succeed Pius XI in March of 1939, though the cardinal secretary of state had served as papal nuncio in Germany from 1917 to 1929.

And

The day after his election, the Berlin *Morgenpost* said: "The election of cardinal Pacelli is not accepted with favour in Germany because he was always opposed to Nazism and practically determined the policies of the Vatican under his predecessor."[7]

If anybody knew about the Vatican's views on German fascism and the personal policies of the man who would become Pope Pius XII, it was of course that very Nazi government. Berlin worked hard to try to prevent the election of Pacelli to the papacy, because he was known to be the main advisor to the Pope on Nazism and to have shaped much of the anti-Nazi policies of the Vatican. Pacelli himself made more than forty speeches in Germany condemning Nazism; spoke, wrote, and broadcast against Hitler's ideas long before the Austrian came to power in 1933; and refused to ever meet the Nazi leader.

While we often hear today that the papacy was indifferent to Jewish suffering and to the rise and ambitions of the Nazis, the Reich's Security Service had an extremely different point of view and gave their informed opinion of the newly elected Pope in 1939. "Pacelli has already made himself prominent by his attacks on National Socialism during his tenure as Cardinal Secretary of State, a fact which earned him the hearty approval of the Democratic States during the papal elections." His first encyclical was *Summi Pontificatus*, which condemned

Nazism and stated, quoting St. Paul, that in the Catholic Church there is "neither Gentile nor Jew, circumcision nor uncircumcision." Joachim Von Ribbentrop, Berlin's most persuasive diplomat, was another contemporary witness. He made a visit to see Pope Pius and told the Pope that Germany would certainly win the war, that the Vatican was being foolish to support the western Allies, and that any defeat of Nazism was a victory for Communism. The Pope listened quietly while Von Ribbentrop spoke and then produced a large folder that listed numerous persecutions, atrocities, and illegalities carried out by the Nazis. He read them out calmly and in perfect German. The meeting was over.[8]

One of the many accusations made against the Pope is that he did not publicly denounce anti-Semitism during the Holocaust. Yet explicit condemnations of Nazi anti-Semitism were not really made in London, Washington, or Moscow, but it's always assumed that Rome should somehow have been different, in spite of the fact that the Vatican was surrounded by Nazi or pro-Nazi troops and that millions of Roman Catholics lived under Nazi occupation, whereas London, Washington, and even Moscow were relatively cocooned and even comparatively safe. The truth is that the Pope did indeed make several condemnations of Nazi racism, both before and during the war – the latter being extremely dangerous and courageous. A public statement, however, was not without consequences and was not at all guaranteed to achieve the desired outcome. One particularly repugnant case of the tragedy of this, and something that influenced the papal position, was what occurred in Holland when the Archbishop of Utrecht preached against the Nazi treatment of Dutch Jews. He had been ordered not to do so, but decided that he had no option. In direct response, the Nazis rounded up not only Jews but Jewish converts to Catholicism, including the Carmelite nun and noted philosopher Edith Stein, who was to die at Auschwitz concentration camp and later to be named as a Catholic saint. In his vitally important book *Three Popes and the Jews*, the Jewish theologian, historian, and Israeli diplomat Pinchas E. Lapide recounts the case of a German Jewish family who managed to escape their homeland for neutral Spain. Like many others, they were able to escape death due to the intervention of the Pope and his staff. They wrote,

> None of us wanted the Pope to take an open stand. We were all fugitives, and fugitives do not wish to be pointed at. The Gestapo would have become more excited and would have intensified its inquisitions. If the Pope had protested, Rome would have become the center of attention. It was better that the Pope said nothing. We all shared this opinion at the time, and this is still our conviction today.

When the Nazis occupied Rome, the papacy and German troops were, quite literally, within each other's sight. We now know that Hitler had made plans to kidnap Pius. In 1943, the Pope may not have been aware of this, but he certainly knew that the Germans were prepared to use force to enter the Vatican, and had murdered Catholic clerics and leaders all over Europe. The context says so much when we consider the Pope's reaction to the Nazi policy toward the Jews of Rome. First, in September 1943, the Germans demanded one hundred pounds of gold within three days or three hundred Jews would be arrested. The Jewish community could raise only two-thirds of the gold, so turned to the Church. Pope Pius smuggled the city's Chief Rabbi into the city and had him taken straight to the Vatican treasury, where he was given what he needed. Tragically, and typically, the payment only postponed the inevitable.

When it became known that the Nazis intended to round up and deport Rome's Jews, the Pope became probably the most active protector of the Jewish people of any regional dignitary in occupied Europe throughout the Second World War. Between four thousand and seven thousand Jews were hidden in almost two hundred refuges in Vatican City. Monasteries, churches, private homes, hospitals, and offices were used, and the Pope gave a personal order that everything must be done to make sure as many Jewish people as possible were sheltered from the Nazis. This included the use of Castel Gandolfo, the Pope's summer residence. Pinchas Lapide again:

> In Rome we saw a list of 155 convents and monasteries –
> Italian, French, Spanish, English, American, and also German
> – mostly extraterritorial property of the Vatican . . . which
> sheltered throughout the German occupation some 5,000
> Jews in Rome. No less than 3,000 Jews found refuge at one
> time at the Pope's summer residence at Castel Gandolfo; sixty
> lived for nine months at the Jesuit Gregorian University, and
> half a dozen slept in the cellar of the Pontifical Bible Institute.

He also concluded after exhaustive research that Pius XII's Roman Catholic Church was more successful and active in rescuing and saving Jews than any other organization in Europe.[9]

Yet still the accusations of collaboration or at least the claims that the Pope did too little continued. Sir Martin Gilbert is one of the most respected historians in the world and a central voice in studies of the Holocaust and Israel. He wrote,

As a historian of the Holocaust I frequently receive requests from Jewish educators, seeking support for grant applications for their Holocaust programs. Almost all these applications include a sentence about how the new program will inform students that the Pope, and the Vatican, "did nothing" during the Holocaust to help Jews. The most recent such portrayal reached me while I was writing this review. It is part of a proposal to a major Jewish philanthropic organization, and contains the sentence: "Also discusses the role of the Vatican and the rabidly anti-Semitic Pope Pius XII, who were privy to information regarding the heinous crimes being committed against the Jews, and their indifferent response." That the Pope and the Vatican were either silent bystanders, or even active collaborators in Hitler's diabolical plan – and "rabidly anti-Semitic," as stated above – has become something of a truism in Jewish educational circles, and a powerful, emotional assertion made by American-Jewish writers, lecturers, and educators.

Gilbert acknowledged the Church's failings, but stressed that, for example,

> in France, leaders of the Roman Catholic clergy were outspoken in their condemnation of the deportations. In Italy, churchmen across the whole spectrum of Roman Catholicism, including leading Jesuits, saved Jews from deportation. Many hundreds of Polish priests and nuns are among more than 5,000 Catholic Poles who have been recognized by the state of Israel for their courage in saving Jews.

He continued,

Among Roman Catholic clergymen who helped save Jews was Archbishop Giovanni Montini, the future Pope Paul VI. When the government of Israel asked him, in 1955, to accept an award for his rescue work during the Holocaust, Montini replied: "All I did was my duty. And besides I only acted upon orders from the Holy Father." When the deportation of 80,000 Jews from Slovakia to Auschwitz began in March 1942, Pius authorized formal written protests by both the Vatican secretary of state and the papal representative in the Slovak capital, Bratislava. When a second round of deportations began in Slovakia the following spring, Pius wrote a letter of protest to the Slovak government. Dated April 7, 1943, it was outspoken and unambiguous. "The Holy See has always entertained the firm hope," Pius wrote, that the Slovak government "would never proceed with the forcible removal of persons belonging to the Jewish race. It is, therefore, with great pain that the Holy See has learned of the continued transfers of such a nature from the territory of the republic."[10]

Arguably the best and most comprehensive book about the Pope Pius controversy was written by Rabbi David G. Dalin in 2005. In *The Myth of Hitler's Pope* he writes poignantly,

Very few of the many recent books about Pius XII and the Holocaust are actually about Pius XII and the Holocaust. The liberal bestselling attacks on the pope and the Catholic Church are really an intra-Catholic argument about the direction of the Church today. The Holocaust is simply the biggest club available for liberal Catholics to use against traditional Catholics in their attempt to bash the papacy and thereby to smash traditional Catholic teaching.

This is very much to the point and can be extended not just to anti-papal Catholics offended by the new orthodoxy of the Church, but to anti-Catholics in greater society. What better way to marginalize a belief and an institution than by alleging that in one of the great battles of good against evil that institution was on the wrong side?

In a 2001 interview with the Vatican newspaper *L'Osservatore Romano*, Dalin stated,

Pope Pacelli was righteous among the nations, who must be recognized for having protected and saved hundreds of thousands of Jews. It is difficult to imagine that so many world Jewish leaders, in such different continents, could have been mistaken or confused when it came to praising the Pope's conduct during the War. Their gratitude to Pius XII lasted a long time, and it was genuine and profound.

As this book was being completed, Dr. Michael Hesemann, a German historian carrying out research in the Vatican archives for the American inter-faith group Pave the Way Foundation, issued some of his findings and announced that "Pope Pius may have arranged the exodus of about 200,000 Jews from Germany just three weeks after Kristallnacht, when thousands of Jews were rounded up and sent to concentration camps."

Commenting on the research, the chairman of the foundation, Elliot Hershberg, said:

Cardinal Eugenio Pacelli – the future Pius XII – wrote to Roman Catholic archbishops around the world to urge them to apply for visas for "non-Aryan Catholics" and Jewish converts to Christianity who wanted to leave Germany. We believe that many Jews who were successful in leaving Europe may not have had any idea that their visas and travel documents were obtained through these Vatican efforts . . . . Everything we have found thus far seems to indicate the known negative perception of Pope Pius XII is wrong.

Surely the final answer to this *canard* is the number and suffering of the Christian victims of Nazism, and the ranks of people persecuted not because they were Christian socialists, Christian anti-Nazis, or Jewish converts to Christianity, but solely and exclusively because they were Christians. In November 2006, a sculpture was unveiled in Germany to remember just the Catholic priests and monks who were slaughtered in one death camp. Ninety-six clergy were killed in Sachsenhausen, a fairly small German camp in Germany, and so far historians have recorded the names of more than eight hundred clergy, mostly German and Polish, who were held in the camp, facing torture and starvation. This was just one, relatively minor camp. In a particularly moving scene, one priest who had suffered terribly in the hell-hole walked forward to thank those present for the memorial; he had survived, become a bishop, and lived long enough to see the sacrifice and martyrdom of his friends remembered. Tragically, forgetting and ignoring is more common than commemoration and concern. It is as though there is a deliberate campaign to ignore the hundreds of thousands, even millions, of Christian clergy and activists who were killed in Nazism's pagan destruction of all and everybody who stood in their way.

In the first weeks of December 1940 alone in Poland, the Nazis arrested 1,997 Catholic priests. Another 1,500 would be arrested and put into concentration camps during the war.

These numbers do not, however, reveal how many priests and monks were simply shot in their churches and homes, such as the 162 French priests arrested by the Gestapo in February 1944, 123 of whom were executed within days. The Nuremburg Trials heard numerous cases of the mass murder of Christians, and particularly Christian leaders. For example, 780 priests died as slave labourers in Mauthausen alone. Some of the individual cases are particularly moving, such as that of Titus Brandsma, a Carmelite priest and internationally respected intellectual and academic, who worked tirelessly against the Nazis both before and after they occupied his homeland of Holland. He was arrested by the Germans and killed with a lethal injection in July 1942. Before he died, he gave his rosary to the ss doctor who had administered the procedure.[11]

Dietrich Bonhoeffer was a Protestant leader, a Lutheran pastor, and a theologian. What is so startling about his death at the hands of the Nazis in 1945 is that it was entirely avoidable. He was safely out of the country and could easily have stayed abroad for the duration of the war – few would have thought any less of him. Instead, he returned to Germany and worked as part of the anti-Nazi resistance before he was arrested and then hanged. He was joined by numerous other Protestant and Catholic men and women in Germany, who gave their freedom, and often their lives, to oppose Hitler. Many of them were conservative, all of them devout, and they were motivated solely by their belief in the Gospels. Indeed the number of German resisters who were Christian is disproportionate when compared to the socialists, Communists, and others who took a stand against National Socialism.

The same pattern emerged throughout occupied Europe. Under the leadership of the Protestant clergymen André Trocmé and Edouard Theis, the people of Chambon-sur-Lignon saved five thousand Jewish people from the death camps. This French Protestant town took the collective decision as a Christian community to stand up against the Nazis and their local collaborators, and do the Christian thing. Elizabeth Koenig-Kaufman, a former child refugee in the town, wrote:

> Nobody asked who was Jewish and who was not. Nobody asked where you were from. Nobody asked who your father was or if you could pay. They just accepted each of us, taking us in with warmth, sheltering children, often without their parents – children who cried in the night from nightmares.

Everybody in the village risked death and torture on a daily basis, but their Christian convictions outweighed their fear.

It is difficult to come even close to paying justice to the vast number of Christians throughout Europe who stood firm against Hitler when he was at his most powerful. To claim that the Nazi founder was a Christian, to argue that Nazism was Christian, to fail to understand and appreciate the inspiring and enormous work of Christians – sometimes alone and detested – in opposing Nazism, is not only anti-historical and foolish, but also downright insulting. It is easy to produce quotations taken out of context to try to prove a fallacy, and simple to misread history, but it is a disservice to truth. It was the Christian author G.K. Chesterton who wrote,

> Not only is suicide a sin, it is *the* sin. It is the ultimate and absolute evil, the refusal to take an interest in existence; the refusal to take the oath of loyalty to life. The man who kills

a man, kills a man. The man who kills himself, kills all men; as far as he is concerned he wipes out the world.

Hitler, Himmler, Goering, Goebbels, and many of the other Nazi leaders took their own lives. They rejected God's law and Christ's teaching in their lives, and in their deaths.

VI

CHRISTIANS AND
CHRISTIANITY SUPPORTED SLAVERY

THE TITLE OF THIS CHAPTER claims two different and separate things. Have people who have described themselves as Christians ever supported slavery? Of course they have. Just as people who have called themselves pretty much everything have been enlightened and reactionary, good and bad. One of the recurring themes of this book is how we need to distinguish between what is done because of, and in spite of, Christianity, and the importance of understanding the separate and distinct nature of Christian teaching, and what individual Christians do and how they behave. The important, underlying argument is, does an intelligent and informed understanding of Christianity lead a person to be an advocate of slavery and all of the injustice and inequality that it involves? Implicit in the slavery debate, of course, and invariably close behind the arguments made against Christians concerning slavery, is the assumption that the enslavement of one group of people by another is necessarily white and Western. In other words, the slavers were British, French, Dutch, Spanish, Portuguese, American, and so on, and the slaves were black Africans. Yet this was only one form of slavery, albeit one of the most organized and cruel. But most cultures had at one time or another taken and used slaves, and even within Africa itself slave economies had been common and were not, as is often suggested, merely the result of internecine war and the subsequent prisoners of war that were taken. In fact, rather than slaves being produced as a result of war and victory or defeat, wars were sometimes waged exclusively to procure slaves. Romans enslaved conquered peoples, as did those conquered peoples when they were themselves triumphant. Most ancient peoples did not even consider skin colour when they took slaves. Power and citizenship and not race and colour were the qualifications for slavery and ownership. Slaves were also sometimes multi-generational, and while some were treated with hideous cruelty, others were sometimes treated with relative compassion. When Britain abolished slavery – due to the efforts, as we shall see, largely of evangelical Christians – the Royal Navy and British army were frequently used to subdue African tribal leaders who insisted on continuing to enslave other tribes, long after Christian Britain had decided that it was morally repugnant. It's also the case that slavery continues today in some parts of the Islamic world, as it always has within Muslim culture, and indeed Islam has a far more worrying and ambivalent attitude toward slavery than does Christianity, witnessed by both Koranic text and the precedents of Muslim history.

One of the factors that distinguished European slavery, however, was its racial nature, and this cannot and should never be denied. While there were black slave traders who captured and sold slaves to Europeans, and while Europeans were certainly enslaved by the Turks well into the seventeenth century, what we think of as the slave trade was an enormously profitable operation organized and controlled by white Christians, and the victims were black African non-Christians. So what should we construe from this? It could be argued that Europeans and Americans used slaves because they were Christians and their religion encouraged them to do so, but that is an anachronistic and tendentious point of view that doesn't stand up to serious scrutiny. It is far more accurate to conclude that men used slaves because they *could* use slaves; in other words, that they were powerful enough, had the means to do so, and acted according to the attitudes of the age and to their will rather than according to the Christian faith.

It's surely a self-evident truth in the opening years of the twenty-first century that slavery is an intolerable evil. Also self-evident is that earlier cultures did not share this opinion and that even the most sophisticated of them, of all races and religions, thought it inevitable and even ethical that the powerful would and should enslave those whom they defeated or those who could not effectively resist capture. One culture and one religion, however, stands out as being virtually unique in condemning and concluding slavery, not when it was impossible not to do so, but when it was easier and far more lucrative to have continued to enslave. The culture is Anglo-Saxon and the religion is Christianity. Those dead white males weren't quite as bad as we like to think. But Europeans certainly enslaved Africans, often buying them from local African warlords or simply transforming local customs into something far more repugnant and far more widespread. There can be, must be, no denial here, because there is no doubt that the white use of black men, women, and children as slaves was organized, brutal, and grotesque. And also enormously profitable. Which makes the grand, great, and prolonged opposition to slavery by the 1780s so profoundly impressive. To put it simply, there was a great deal to lose, there was nothing to gain, and there was no pressing or practical need to change anything. The only dynamic and moral force behind the series of boycotts of slave-produced products, the campaigns to expose the cruelty of slavery, and the eventually successful legislation to abolish that trade, was that in Christian eyes it was considered *wrong*. There were certainly church figures who supported slavery, but there were also people from all areas of life who supported it. What is important is that with a few exceptions, the only committed and dedicated opponents of the slave trade were monks, priests, and Christian laity. Secular and non-Christian resistance was rare, and for entire generations almost unheard of.

This opposition, and not the urge to convert people, was often one of the major reasons why Christian missionaries were so vehemently opposed by many African chieftains. The famous Dr. Livingstone, described in chapter 8, "Christians and Progress," at greater length, spent much of his time in central Africa preaching against slavery, much to the chagrin of the local Arab slave-dealers, and their indigenous partners, who made a fortune out of selling Africans to other parts of the continent and to the Middle East. The Sultan of Zanzibar was forced to end slavery as late as 1873 when the British arrived. In an act that would today be called barbarically imperialistic the British occupiers went so far as to build an Anglican cathedral on the site of the destroyed slave market. In 1843, the British took Karachi in modern-day Pakistan from its Muslim leaders and demanded that the slave trade be stopped immediately and that the slave market be razed to the ground. The British, Christian liberators built in its place a huge fruit and vegetable market to help feed the local people, one that operates to this day. The notion that Islam rejects slavery and Christianity encourages it is, frankly, laughable.[1]

What is extremely clear if we read contemporary records and accounts, is that after the British abolished slavery in the early nineteenth century, and other Europeans and the Americans followed suit within a further fifty years, in the eyes of many African and Arab leaders Christian expansion signified an end to slavery, which is one of the reasons why British ships so regularly battled Muslim pirates around North Africa and why Anglo-Celtic culture was seen as a liberating force by contemporary liberal movements. By the 1830s, the real axis of evil that was slavery connected Africa, south Asia, and Arabia, and lasted far longer than it had in the white, Christian world. Indeed, it still exists. According to anti-slavery groups, there are still millions of people who are enslaved servants and concubines, thus being little better off than slaves and sometimes literally enslaved. In Sudan, Animist and Christian tribes were until recently and to an extent still are, raided by Arab militias; the men are killed and the women and children taken as slaves. There are cane workers in leg shackles in southern Pakistan, and hundreds of thousands of women and children are sold from Benin and Togo to wealthier African nations such as Nigeria and Gabon. The criminals who operate these multinational enterprises are seldom reprimanded, and in the case of Sudan were applauded and supported by numerous Islamic states that profited from their illegal activities. They must be incredulous at the post-Christian Westerners beating their breasts and crying for forgiveness for something their ancestors worked so hard to stop. Those ancestors did so only because their Christian faith and European enlightenment convinced them that it was wrong. How jaundiced we are by the incarceration of our time, and how little we understand of the past.

The Christian world also knew a few things about the evils of slavery long before the eighteenth-century campaign to abolish it. In 1537, Pope Paul III issued a Papal Bull on the issue of natives, slavery, and the relationship between conqueror and conquered in the New World, who were not, of course, Christian. In that a Papal Bull is a formal and profoundly authoritative document, this is an extraordinarily significant piece of evidence as to the Christian approach to slavery as early as the Renaissance.

We define and declare by these Our letters, or by any translation thereof signed by any notary public and sealed with the seal of any ecclesiastical dignitary, to which the same credit shall be given as to the originals, that, notwithstanding whatever may have been or may be said to the contrary, the said Indians and all other people who may later be discovered by Christians, are by no means to be deprived of their liberty or the possession of their property, even though they be outside the faith of Jesus Christ; and that they may and should, freely and legitimately, enjoy their liberty and the possession of their property; nor should they be in any way enslaved; should the contrary happen, it shall be null and have no effect. By virtue of Our apostolic authority We define and declare by these present letters, or by any translation thereof signed by any notary public and sealed with the seal of any ecclesiastical dignitary, which shall thus command the same obedience as the originals, that the said Indians and other peoples should be converted to the faith of Jesus Christ by preaching the word of God and by the example of good and holy living.

It is William Wilberforce, however, who stands out most clearly as having been the Christian voice of opposition to the slave trade. This diminutive, often unhealthy, but intellectually gifted man was MP for Hull in Yorkshire, northern England. He was a social creature, a man who enjoyed gossip and parties and the good things in life. He was also a close friend of the future prime minister, William Pitt, and was thought to be a "coming man," destined for political greatness. His greatness was to be achieved in a different field though, and his fame internationally is far greater than that of his friend Pitt. In adult life, he underwent a conversion to what we would now consider evangelical

Christianity, and his life was transformed. Friends thought that he had had some sort of breakdown, as he put his past life behind him, began to give money away, and opened up his home to the poor. He told these friends that there was no need to worry, and that his two ambitions were now to change the manner – what we would call the morals – of England, and to end the slave trade. Which made them even more concerned, as this was audacious to the point of lunacy, something that those friends lost no time in pointing out. But he was not to be dissuaded. In his own words:

> Is it not the great end of religion, and, in particular, the glory of Christianity, to extinguish the malignant passions; to curb the violence, to control the appetites, and to smooth the asperities of man? To make us compassionate and kind, and forgiving one to another; to make us good husbands, good fathers, good friends; and to render us active and useful in the discharge of the relative social and civil duties?[2]

Wilberforce gathered a group of like-minded devoted Christians, men and women who were committed to Gospel-based social justice, and who were willing to give their lives if necessary to live out God's word and instructions. Wilberforce wrote:

> Accustom yourself to look first to the dreadful conse-quences of failure; then fix your eye on the glorious prize which is before you; and when your strength begins to fail, and your spirits are well nigh exhausted, let the animating view rekindle your resolution, and call forth in renewed vigour the fainting energies of your soul.[3]

The anti-slavery movement effectively began in Britain in 1787 with a meeting of twelve Christians who were experienced in social action, including Wilberforce. Some of the other driving characters behind the movement were Thomas Clarkson – "We cannot suppose therefore that God has made an order of beings, with such mental qualities and powers, for the sole purpose of being used as beasts, or instruments of labour" – along with the converted slave trader and author of "Amazing Grace," John Newton, and the members of the Clapham Sect.

The Clapham Sect, a group of evangelical Anglicans who met in the London district of Clapham, dedicated themselves to slavery abolition, to prison reform, and to the relief of the poor. They were strongly encouraged by Beilby Porteus, who was the Anglican bishop of London, and they went on to publish the *Christian Observer* journal and were deeply involved with Bible translation work and the distribution of Christian tracts in numerous languages throughout the world. Dr. Thomas Sowell, the black columnist and author, makes an interesting point when he says,

> The anti-slavery movement was spearheaded by people who would today be called "the religious right" and its organization was created by conservative businessmen. Moreover, what destroyed slavery in the non-Western world was Western imperialism.

To put it another way, these Christians knew that the British empire had helped to establish slavery, and they were intent as believers to use that British empire to eradicate the slavery they as Christians so despised, and in so doing spread the Gospel of Christ. It's jarring to secular and anti-Christian ears, but that does not mean that it isn't true.

It's also comforting to the modern mentality eager to find fault with Christianity to point out that half a century after Britain had abolished slavery, it was still practised in the southern part of the United States, a region heavily committed to Protestant Christianity. More than this, the conventional wisdom today is that contrary to what we used to think, the American Civil War was not waged to end slavery but to impose the influence of Washington and the north on the Confederacy and on a south obsessed with states' rights. The Civil War, we are told, had little to do with the emancipation of the slaves. Sweeping statements are seldom accurate, and motives are rarely completely pure. The abolitionist movement was a central influence in accentuating the division of the country, and the desire to end slavery from Christian activists was a massive factor in eventually leading to the outbreak of war. Of course there were many other political and economic issues involved, but we know from letters, diaries, and speeches made at the time that emancipation and racial justice permeated the Union position and the northern point of view and this ideology was almost wholly created, led by, and organized by Christians.

Indeed, evangelical Christians had been campaigning for an end to slavery long before the Civil War and had applied political and social pressure before and during the American Revolution, and even as early as the 1760s. In the first years of the next century, Benjamin Lundy led a movement of Quakers and other Christians to abolish slavery in America, and to provide an alternative home for freed slaves. He began and edited an abolitionist newspaper, leading directly to the work of the Presbyterian minister Lyman Beecher and the Calvinist theologian Nathaniel Taylor in New England. This in turn led to religious revivals, campaigns for moral reform, and specific anti-slavery activism from Charles G. Finney, and then Theodore D. Weld, and then Arthur Tappan and his brother Lewis. Arthur and Lewis Tappan were the founders, with William Lloyd Garrison, of the anti-slavery publication *The Liberator*, and with other Christians were the driving force behind the origins of the American Anti-Slavery Society, founded in Philadelphia in 1833.[4]

Within two years, members of this overwhelmingly Christian organization were petitioning Congress, touring both the north and the south, often at great physical risk, and publishing pamphlets and leaflets. They were met with political as well as personal hostility in the slave states and even outside of the South, with Congress imposing a gag rule so as to be able to ignore their petitions, and abolitionist leaders being followed to their homes and churches, and members of their family being warned to stop their campaigns or face violence or death. It was much more than empty words, and in 1837 Elijah Parish Lovejoy, the editor of one of the most important anti-slavery newspapers, was murdered by an enraged mob of slavery supporters in Alton, Illinois. Just five days before his death, the Presbyterian minister had given a speech in the same town where he would be martyred, in which he explained the Christian imperative behind the battle against slavery:

It is not true, as has been charged upon me, that I hold in contempt the feelings and sentiments of this community, in reference to the question which is now agitating it. I respect and appreciate the feelings and opinions of my fellow-citizens, and it is one of the most painful and unpleasant duties of my life, that I am called upon to act in opposition to them. If you suppose, sir, that I have published sentiments contrary to those generally held in this community, because I delighted in differing from them, or in occasioning a disturbance, you have entirely misapprehended me. But, sir, while I value the good opinion of my fellow-citizens, as highly as any one, I may be permitted to say, that I am governed by higher considerations than either the favor or the fear of man. I am impelled to the course I have taken, because I fear God. As I shall answer it to my God in the great day, I dare not abandon my sentiments, or cease in all proper ways to propagate them.

He concluded with

I have concluded, after consultation with my friends, and earnestly seeking counsel of God, to remain at Alton, and here to insist on protection in the exercise of my rights. If the civil authorities refuse to protect me, I must look to God; and if I die, I have determined to make my grave in Alton.[5]

In an example of a quintessentially Christian paradox, his death gave greater life to the abolitionist movement, and within a year there were more than 1,350 anti-slavery societies in the country, boasting more than 225,000 members. Throughout the 1840s and 1850s, churches were filled with abolitionist speakers and activists, with enormous pressure brought to play on politicians. There were certainly Christians and even entire churches and denominations that rejected the anti-slavery movement, but the point is that the only people and the only leaders willing to give all for the cause were Christians. This statement may lead people to quote various passages from the Bible without context and understanding, and ignoring the historical narrative completely, to argue that actually the Bible condones slavery.

First, we need to realize that the Christian views the Old Testament through the prism of the New. The Old Testament can only be understood properly once we know its conclusion, once we know what happened, and know what God had planned in the Bible's completeness. Otherwise, it would be like trying to understand a novel without reading its final chapters, watching a race but turning away before it ends. It would make no sense. So any difficulties within the Old Testament are more properly asked of Judaism, but that would not help Christian-bashers at all. Beyond this, though, the Old Testament is by no means as obtuse and difficult as some people suggest, if we make the effort.

Slavery has existed in all ages and in all cultures, usually without any prohibitions or moral stipulations. So when the book of Leviticus demands compassionate and gentle care and treatment of every person under a man's authority, it is positively revolutionary. The Jews of the Old Testament were told to treat their slaves as members of the family; they were to be protected from physical abuse, and to be included in the family's religious worship, and – vital, this – the family's wealth and possessions. Not at all like the slavery of other cultures, and that of the European enslavement of Africans. In fact, not like slavery as we know it. The Old Testament also told the Jewish people to eventually release their slaves, returning them to their place of origin, and guaranteeing that they had enough money and resources to restart their lives. Not quite the hideous caricature we have been led to believe is the Old Testament's advice on enslavement.

The New Testament itself does not judge slavery explicitly, but then Jesus and His followers do not explicitly condemn any number of things that they clearly considered repugnant. Sometimes immorality and evil are self-evident, so much so that comment is redundant. Jesus does not condemn infanticide, ethnic cleansing, or cannibalism, for example, but we can be pretty sure where He stood on the issues. What the New Testament does emphasize is that God expects every person to live good, ethical, and empathetic lives, and this should lead inexorably and inevitably to a resistance to slavery. We know that the Romans had freed many of their slaves and given them their complete freedom in the second and third centuries, almost certainly under the influence of an increasingly influential Christian community and under pressure from influential converts to Christianity. There are almost a hundred references to slavery in the New Testament, and – again – while Christ does not demand an end to slavery, we have to realize that for an often impoverished and illiterate population, slavery or something approaching it was the only alternative to starvation and death. So, while the New Testament does presume that slavery will sometimes have to exist, it makes it quite clear what the Christian approach to slavery should be.

First Corinthians says,

> For by one Spirit we were all baptized into one body, whether Jews or Greeks, whether slaves or free, and we were all made to drink of one Spirit,

and Second Corinthians,

> For we do not preach ourselves but Christ Jesus as Lord, and ourselves as your bond-servants for Jesus' sake.

In Ephesians we see,

> Slaves, be obedient to those who are your masters according
> to the flesh, with fear and trembling, in the sincerity of your
> heart, as to Christ,

but this is qualified shortly afterwards with

> Not by way of eye service, as men-pleasers, but as slaves of
> Christ, doing the will of God from the heart. With good will
> render service, as to the Lord, and not to men, knowing that
> whatever good thing each one does, this he will receive back
> from the Lord, whether slave or free. And masters, do the
> same things to them, and give up threatening, knowing that
> both their Master and yours is in heaven, and there is no par-
> tiality with Him.

In other words, masters are to treat slaves not really as slaves at
all, which is emphasized in Colossians with this:

> Masters, grant to your slaves justice and fairness, knowing
> that you too have a Master in heaven.

So what are we to conclude? The Christian world abolished slavery, while slavery still exists in certain Islamic nations,
and slavery in all but name is extraordinarily common in
Communist states such as China and North Korea. It was
Franciscans who tried to prevent slavery in Latin America
when it was conquered by Spain, it was Quakers and evangelical Anglicans who fought for slavery to be abolished in Britain
and the British empire, Calvinists who gave so much to abolish
slavery in the United States. Even today, the campaign to end
slavery where it still exists is very much a Christian enterprise.

John Brown's body "lies a-mouldering in the grave, but his soul goes marching on." Well, it does, but the fiery abolitionist would be stunned to know that the modern world often doesn't even know that he, his comrades, and the less violent but equally determined foes of slavery were all Christians. Sorry, John.

VII

THE IDEA THAT CHRISTIANITY IS SOMEHOW opposed to science, and that individual Christians cannot reconcile their faith to scientific discoveries, is a relatively modern *canard*, but successfully and damagingly promulgated, usually by people who know very little about science and its history, or about Christianity and Christians. It's a part of the larger, "Christians are stupid" approach, usually offered by people who are inspired by talk shows rather than texts, and assume that because a television mini-series or popular novel has depicted Christians as being superstitious, foolish, reactionary, and frightened of change, such must be the case. The science aspect of all this is particularly nauseating, not only because it is fundamentally untrue, but that it is thrown at Christianity at a time when society is arguably experiencing one of its most credulous and naive stages and is only too willing to embrace any and every kind of non-scientific or anti-scientific nonsense, from alien invasion stories to ghost myths, and from conspiracy theories to supernatural animals. To paraphrase the great Christian writer G.K. Chesterton, when people stop believing in God, they don't believe in something else, they believe in *anything* else.

The Elizabethan and Jacobean politician and philosopher, Sir Francis Bacon, himself a scientist, writing in *Of Atheism*, stated,

It is true, that a little philosophy inclineth man's mind to atheism, but depth in philosophy bringeth men's minds about to religion; for while the mind of man looketh upon second causes scattered, it may sometimes rest in them, and go no further; but when it beholdeth the chain of them confederate, and linked together, it must needs fly to Providence and Deity.

It's a pithy and acutely observant remark that applies even more bitingly to the twenty-first century than to the late sixteenth and early seventeenth. Bacon, by the way, is sometimes used by modern atheists as an example of an anti-Christian, perhaps because of his possible homosexuality. But it's untrue, and his work in science as well as in philosophy was always, he claimed, undertaken to aid his country, his faith, and the truth.[1]

The point about Bacon, however, is not that he was as a Christian and a scientist a rare commodity, but that such a combination was and is entirely typical. It is estimated that the majority of academics working in the scientific field in the world's major universities today believe in God, and that many of those believers are Christian. The blurred vision, the distorted image, of Christianity and science being contradictory, at war with one another, or mutually exclusive, is largely a recent construct, emerging from the battle between modernism and traditionalism in the United States in the early twentieth century. The new school of rationalism and secularism that informed, or infected, scientific debate at this period pushed some of the more raw evangelical theologians and leaders, and particularly those on the Protestant fundamentalist wing, into something of an intellectual ghetto. Or to put it another way, slid them into a distinctly anti-intellectual mode. But they were and remain a small minority within world Christianity, albeit a minority with a loud voice, and one that is listened to all too readily and eagerly by a media anxious to discredit Christianity.[2]

The history of Christianity is actually one of great encouragement of scientific research and has been responsible for many of the most important scientific advances. A contemporary of Bacon's was Johannes Kepler, another devout Christian, who was one of the most original and influential astronomers and mathematicians of all time, and certainly of his era. His scientific work in the areas of light and how we understand it changed the fundamentals of scientific research. He established the laws of planetary motion about the sun, and this observant and committed Lutheran was close to giving us the laws of gravity a century before they would be formed. The man who actually did form those laws was another pious Christian, Sir Isaac Newton. One of the two or three most important physicists in history, he was a dominant figure in mathematics, astronomy, and so many aspects of scientific study. What is not always remembered – or is deliberately obscured – is that his fascination for numbers was largely inspired by his fascination with God's plan for the universe. In *Principia* he wrote, "The most beautiful system of the sun, planets, and comets, could only proceed from the counsel and dominion of an intelligent and powerful Being."

Newton was followed by numerous Christians engaged in scientific study in the eighteenth century, but in the middle of the seventeenth came Robert Boyle, one of the founders of the Royal Society in Britain. While known for giving his name to Boyle's Law, he was first a dedicated Protestant who donated money to translate the Bible into Turkish and was a major supporter of attempts to convert Muslims to Christianity. In his book *The Christian Virtuoso*, published in 1690, he wrote:

Most rational men scruple not to believe, upon competent testimony, many things, whose truth did no way appear to them by the consideration of the nature of the things themselves, nay, though what is thus believed upon the testimony be so strange, and, setting aside that testimony, would *seem so irrational*, that, antecedently to that testimony, . . . concerning things merely natural or civil, whereof of human reason is held to be a proper judge.

And,

We ought, of all the things that can be recommended to us by testimony, to receive those of the highest degree of assent, that are taught us by God . . . repose a great deal of trust in the testimony of inspired persons, such as Christ and his apostles.

Closer to the modern age is Michael Faraday, who although from a working-class background as the son of a blacksmith, became one of the most respected scientists of the nineteenth century. He specialized in the fields of electricity and magnetism, his discoveries saved many lives, and he was one of the researchers who formed the bases for later developments in computer science. He was also a determined and conscientious Christian, and a member of the Sandemanians, an English branch of a Scottish denomination that rejected state or church control and looked to a more independent and Bible-based form of worship. An article in the September 1991 edition of the *New Scientist*, a firmly non-Christian publication, stated:

Faraday found no conflict between his religious beliefs and his activities as a scientist and philosopher. He viewed his discoveries of nature's laws as part of the continual process of *"reading the book of nature,"* no different in principle from the process of reading the Bible to discover God's laws. A strong sense of the unity of God and nature pervaded Faraday's life and work.

William Thomson Kelvin lived into the first years of the twentieth century, when atheism was beginning to gain prestige and power in many British and European universities, and especially in the field of scientific study. Kelvin was an honoured physicist and a revered scientist, giving the world the fundamental science and knowledge that would lead to broadcasting, the telephone, and modern communications. From 1903 until his death in 1907, he was president of the Largs and Fairlie Auxiliary of the National Bible Society of Scotland and was one of the key supporters of the campaign to restore Christianity and Bible knowledge to Scottish education.

Max Planck was awarded the Nobel Prize for Physics in 1918 and is recognized as the father of the quantum theory. His research was revolutionary, transforming our knowledge of the atomic and of the sub-atomic. He came from a family of theologians, was a devout Christian, and was even a church warden for almost thirty years of his life. Planck wrote,

Anybody who has been seriously engaged in scientific work of any kind realizes that over the entrance to the gates of the temple of science are written the words: "Ye must have faith." It is a quality which the scientist cannot dispense with.

And,

There can never be any real opposition between religion and science; for the one is the complement of the other. Every serious and reflective person realizes, I think, that the religious element in his nature must be recognized and cultivated if all the powers of the human soul are to act together in perfect balance and harmony. And indeed it was not by accident that the greatest thinkers of all ages were deeply religious souls.

So the world of science bursts, bulges, with Christians. But none of this matters when some bright spark with a grudge against God and Christianity can mention Galileo. It's the ace in the pack, the big gun, the name to throw out there when all the secular arguments have been lost. Mind you, in my experience most of the people who insist on mentioning Galileo can't actually spell his name correctly, and they certainly have no idea about what actually happened to him, or why it happened in the first place. His case is used over and over again because critics can't think of any other scientists who were mistreated by either the Catholic or Protestant churches. And in this instance they're right. There may have been some people in the scientific world that did not enjoy Christian support and were even challenged by Christianity, but they were very few. And compared with the number of scientists who were direct beneficiaries of Christianity, the number seems even more insignificant. The Christian Church has been the handmaiden of science and scientific discovery, and those who refer to Galileo tend to forget that Louis Pasteur, the inventor of pasteurization, was a devout Catholic, as was Alexander Fleming, who gave us penicillin. Or Father Nicolaus Copernicus, who first proposed the theory of the earth revolving around the sun – this was precisely what Galileo stated, but Copernicus taught it as theory, not as fact.

Or Monsignor Georges Henri Joseph Édouard Lemaître, a Belgian Roman Catholic priest and professor of physics at the Catholic University of Leuven, who proposed what became known as the Big Bang theory of the origin of the universe. The Big Bang theory, by the way, was opposed by the secular, scientific world when it was first discussed, because it sounded too Christian. Who, then, had the open minds and who the closed?[3]

In the field of acceleration, Father Giambattista Riccioli changed the way we understand that particular science; the father of modern Egyptology was Father Athanasius Kircher, and the Yugoslavian Father Roger Boscovich was the founder of modern atomic theory. The man considered the father of genetics is the great Gregor Mendel. This University of Vienna–trained mathematician conducted a variety of complex experiments in the mid-nineteenth century, the most famous and important of which was when he grew pea plants over an eight-year period and explored their genetic code with great and lasting success in the area of genetics. He was a Catholic monk and later became abbot of his monastery. The Lutheran convert Father Nicholas Steno was one of the founders of geology, and Father J.B. Macelwane's *Introduction to Theoretical Seismology* was the first American textbook on the subject. It was Roman Catholic clergy who took western science to China, India, and Latin America.

Catholic priests as well as Catholic laypeople have joined Protestant thinkers in contributing to science with staggering success. Even before the nineteenth century, the Jesuits in particular, according to Jonathan Wright in his seminal book on the order,

had contributed to the development of pendulum clocks, pantographs, barometers, reflecting telescopes and microscopes, to scientific fields as various as magnetism, optics and electricity. They observed, in some cases before anyone else, the colored bands on Jupiter's surface, the Andromeda nebula and Saturn's rings. They theorized about the circulation of the blood (independently of Harvey), the theoretical possibility of flight, the way the moon affected the tides, and the wave-like nature of light. Star maps of the southern hemisphere, symbolic logic, flood-control measures on the Po and Adige rivers, introducing plus and minus signs into Italian mathematics – all were typical Jesuit achievements, and scientists as influential as Fermat, Huygens, Leibniz and Newton were not alone in counting Jesuits among their most prized correspondents.

So Christianity and science and scientific breakthrough have not been in conflict but lived in mutual regard. It's particularly scandalous that many of the most vocal of those who condemn what they believe to be Christian anti-scientific bigotry are frequently part of a political left that tends to ally itself with an animal rights movement that resists using animals for scientific progress and even threatens or actually attacks scientists who do so.[4]

Which brings us back to Galileo. But what we need to remember is that Galileo was condemned, not because of some scientific breakthrough and not because the Catholic Church – contrary to the modern version of events – was determined to resist change and progress because it feared a loss of power and control. Galileo was challenged because he declared a theory to be a fact and argued with the Church about the genuine meaning of the Bible. In 1992, Pope John Paul II apologized for the Church's treatment of Galileo and described the denunciation as a "tragic error." In 2008, Pope Benedict emphasized the importance of the scientist and praised his achievements. But acknowledgement of past wrongs and contrition are the last things wanted by critics of the Church. Far better to throw the Galileo chant around than listen to an organization explain that in this instance it did not behave according to its usually exemplary standards.

It would be easier if the case was straightforward, but, just like science, it requires a bit of effort to understand. During Galileo's life, the Catholic Church was at the centre of scientific discovery and sponsored scientists both in Rome and throughout the Catholic world, just as was the case before Galileo and would be afterwards. Indeed, Nicolaus Copernicus dedicated his seminal work, *On the Revolution of the Celestial Orbs*, to Pope Paul III. This is important because the book outlined Copernicus's theories concerning heliocentrism. This is the astronomical theory that the earth and other planets revolve around the stationary sun, which is at the centre of the universe. As opposed to geocentrism, which claims the opposite. It wasn't a new idea, having first been proposed as early as the third century B.C. by Aristarchus of Samos. Copernicus was a Catholic and a priest, his brother an Augustinian monk who became a canon, and his sister a Benedictine nun who became a prioress. It wasn't the reaction of the Catholic Church that concerned Copernicus, but the emerging Protestantism of the mid-sixteenth century. While critics claim that the divide between Catholic and Protestant stifled discussion, this is not always the situation at all – in this case as well as others the dialogue produced more discussion and more answers.

None of this is considered when the name and example of Galileo is used to dismiss the Christian Church as reactionary and anti-scientific. The reality is that while heliocentrism was discussed and often accepted within Catholic circles – it was effectively the only place where it could be – the more traditional view of the solar system still prevailed even among leading scientists. So it's hardly a surprise that Galileo's Catholic judges had difficulty accepting his views, especially when they saw themselves as defending scientific orthodoxy and were supported in this by the scientific establishment. Aristotle had rejected heliocentricity and while, as we've seen, Copernicus and Kepler challenged him, they were far ahead of their time and were not always taken seriously by some of the leading scientists of the day. Today we can prove and disprove things with an ease that would have boggled the mind a hundred years ago, let alone in the seventeenth century. It's not only ignorant but supremely arrogant to believe that knowledge is constant. Even Galileo couldn't prove heliocentricity, and in particular failed to counter the very argument that had been made by Aristotle two thousand years earlier. The Greek philosopher's position was that if heliocentrism was indeed true, we would be able to observe it by obvious shifts in the positions of the stars as the earth moved around the sun. Obviously the equipment required to prove this did not exist in the time of Aristotle or Galileo, because of the enormous distance from the earth to the stars. Remember, Christianity's claim is quite specific – not to be an infallible source of wisdom or to know scientific truths long before they have been discovered but to be the body and teaching office founded and left to us by Christ to communicate the Gospel, spread the word of Christianity, and save sinners. That it provided and provides a culture and context for other, secular truths to be propagated is a by-product and not the essence of its existence.[5]

The science of Galileo's time was limited and the entirely reasonable view from intelligent observation was that the earth was not moving at all, but that the sun, moon, and stars were.

Galileo was asked to prove his theory using the best scientific methods of the period, but could not do so. Numerous colleagues thought he had failed. Scientific disagreement was encouraged in the Church and far more radical ideas than those of Galileo had been offered for more than a century. He alienated fellow scientists by his insistence that his observations were true, that they were fact, that they were established, and that any alternative was not only totally wrong but the product of weak thinking and incompetent analysis. Galileo got into trouble because he maintained that since the new discoveries seemed to contradict Scripture, those passages of Scripture should be reinterpreted in a metaphorical way. He did not seek to oppose the Church nor to doubt the inspiration of Scripture. The problem is that he abandoned science and started talking theology and so attracted the notice of the Roman Inquisition. If he had left theology out of his writings and discussions he would probably never have had problems. And he remained a faithful and devout Catholic to the end of his life. Other scientists urged him not to bring theological matters into his writings, not necessarily out of fear, but because they considered it to be hubris on his part – why, they asked, would you make this a matter of faith when the Church has supported and financed your and our work and provided a safe, encouraging environment for scientific research? Priests and bishop friends of Galileo made the same argument: his theory could well be true and, if so, in time it would be accepted as such. But Galileo was not to be turned. This new truth, he said, contradicted scripture.

Pope Paul V met with Galileo and, while not unsympathetic, refused to deal with the matter any further. The Galileo controversy was given to the Holy Office, which officially condemned Galileo's theory in 1616 and hoped that the entire debate would now disappear. It should be stressed that it was Galileo rather than the Church who refused to allow the wound to heal. Cardinal Robert Bellarmine, a Jesuit, a friend of science, and an internationally respected theologian and scholar, tried to reach a compromise when he issued a document that purposely said different things to different people. Galileo, it said, could not hold or argue the position, but could explore and discuss it. It was an attempt to allow Galileo room to work without officially supporting his criticisms of the Church. This remained in place until 1623, when Galileo approached the new Pope, who was an old friend, Urban VIII. Maffeo Barberini had been and remained a patron of the arts and a supporter of scientific investigation. He had long encouraged Galileo, both as a friend and as a cardinal, and now as Pope tried to help him further. He strongly advised Galileo to approach the entire situation extremely carefully and to outline, as a good scholar should, the arguments both for and against the theory. It's never been fully explained why Galileo reacted so churlishly to this sound advice from a man who not only had befriended him, but had defended him as well. Instead of pursuing his work, Galileo appeared to seek confrontation and attempted to humiliate the Pope. In his book *Dialogue on the Two World Systems* he took the Pope's advice to present both sides of the debate, but had Urban's position advocated by the character Simplicio, making fun of the character and the argument and making the Pope a figure of fun in the eyes of the academic world. It is said that Urban was truly hurt and felt betrayed by someone he had trusted and loved. Galileo also attacked the Jesuits and their astronomers, who had gone to great lengths to write and speak in his defence. Galileo was not some innocent, impotent victim standing up for truth and being persecuted by ignorant and violent people, but an activist intent on conflict who repeatedly rejected offers of compromise.

Galileo would eventually publicly recant his views and ostensibly reject heliocentrism but not, as is popularly assumed, because he was tortured. It is astounding how many people, including those who claim some knowledge of history, science, and the Church, make this claim as though it were absolute truth. Galileo was not tortured and was not even treated particularly badly. Ambassador Nicolini, the leading Tuscan diplomat in Rome, was a close friend of Galileo and wrote extensively about the case. If he had a bias, it was in favour of Galileo and against the Vatican. He sent regular reports to the court regarding affairs in Rome. Many of his letters dealt with the ongoing controversy surrounding Galileo, and he reported to his king, "The pope told me that he had shown Galileo a favour never accorded to another" and that "he has a servant and every convenience." The infamous image of a prisoner being shown the instruments of torture is sadly true – it was standard legal practice at the time – but they were not used on Galileo, and not even seriously threatened. As we see if we examine the authentic history of the Inquisition, there were entire books of laws, statutes, and case precedents dealing with what was allowed and not allowed in these cases and *The Directory for Inquisitors* of 1595 prevented torture in such circumstances. If the laws surrounding torture had been broken, those responsible would have faced severe punishment.

The entire Galileo episode reveals both scientist and Christian Church as less than perfect, but says relatively little about the Christianity's attitude toward science. If we want long-term evidence of an ideology controlling and oppressing science, we'd be better off looking to the great atheist regimes of the twentieth century. Stalin actually had his scientists lie about their discoveries to the point where they in turn lied to him, and as a result entire government policy was sometimes based on fraudulent research. The Soviets after Stalin and then under the supposedly more benign rule of Khrushchev and Brezhnev would use psychiatry as a form of torture, incarcerating political dissidents under the guise that they were mentally ill, with the full backing of many in the scientific establishment. The atheist, cultist Hitler was obsessed with the use of science to support his theories of eugenics, social engineering, and so-called racial health. One of the great ironies of the Galileo mess is that the famous play about his life that did so much to portray the Church as evil and terrified of change was written by Bertolt Brecht – a committed and doctrinaire Communist who publicly championed Soviet and East German Communism while free-thinking doctors, scientists, and researchers were being arrested and tortured and medicine used as a tool of the truly dictatorial state.

Let's end this chapter with a few quotations from scientists on the subject, whether they be Christian or not. British astrophysicist Fred Hoyle stated,

A common sense interpretation of the facts suggests that a superintellect has monkeyed with physics, as well as with chemistry and biology, and that there are no blind forces worth speaking about in nature. The numbers one calculates from the facts seem to me so overwhelming as to put this conclusion almost beyond question.

Physicist Paul Davies:

There is for me powerful evidence that there is something going on behind it all . . . . It seems as though somebody has fine-tuned nature's numbers to make the Universe . . . . The impression of design is overwhelming.

NASA astronomer John O'Keefe:

We are, by astronomical standards, a pampered, cosseted, cherished group of creatures . . . . If the Universe had not been made with the most exacting precision we could never have come into existence. It is my view that these circumstances indicate the universe was created for man to live in.

And astronomer George Greenstein:

As we survey all the evidence, the thought insistently arises that some supernatural agency – or, rather, Agency – must be involved. Is it possible that suddenly, without intending to, we have stumbled upon scientific proof of the existence of a Supreme Being? Was it God who stepped in and so providentially crafted the cosmos for our benefit?

From the field of microbiology, University of Illinois academic Carl Woese stated,

Life in Universe – rare or unique? I walk both sides of that street. One day I can say that given the 100 billion stars in our galaxy and the 100 billion or more galaxies, there have to be some planets that formed and evolved in ways very, very like the Earth has, and so would contain microbial life at least.

There are other days when I say that the anthropic principal, which makes this universe a special one out of an unaccountably large number of universes, may not apply only to that aspect of nature we define in the realm of physics, but may extend to chemistry and biology. In that case life on Earth could be entirely unique.

A strong case. Christians have often led in the field of scientific inquiry, both historically and in the present, and there are also non-Christian scientists who are open to God, creation, and Intelligent Design. There is no necessary contradiction between science and faith. How ironic it is that many of those who are most insistent that Christians do not think, and oppose science, are those who do so little thinking about science. There is probably a chemical equation somewhere to explain it, but we have to wait for a Christian to discover it.

VIII

CHRISTIANS OPPOSE PROGRESS AND CHANGE

AS WE SAW IN THE LAST CHAPTER, a large part of the atheist interpretation of history is built on a belief that Christians have generally stood in the way of positive change, and that any progress made is in spite of and not because of Christians or Christianity. If they have produced change, the argument runs, it is purely incidental or even accidental, and not a product of intrinsic Christian belief. So let's look at just a few of the major personalities who propelled the world forward, and analyze the reasons for progress in some specific areas of human improvement, such as health care, prison reform, care for the marginalized, racial equality, and working conditions. We've dealt elsewhere in the book with the struggle against slavery and Nazism, but one of the greatest improvements to the human condition in the past two centuries was in the field of labour and working conditions. Many people have worked on the ongoing project, but one personality tends to stand out. Anthony Ashley Cooper, later to become Lord Shaftesbury in Britain, was a Christian activist who summed up his approach to change and progress with the attitude "Social reforms, so necessary, so indispensable, require as much of God's grace as a change of heart." It's fitting that he attended the funeral of the great William Wilberforce in 1833, because in many ways, and although in a different field, Shaftesbury took up and carried the baton in the same Christian race against injustice.

Anthony Ashley Cooper was born in 1801 in London and enjoyed a privileged background and education, first at the famous Harrow school, and then at Christ Church College, Oxford. His parents were cold and distant – physically as well as emotionally – but he was shown great love and devotion by the family housekeeper Maria Millis, who not only became a surrogate mother to the boy, but also formed him as a Christian with her devout sense of faith and a commitment to Christian social justice. From her, and from his own reading of the Bible, he realized that as he had been given so much, he was duty-bound as a believer, as a follower of Christ, to give much back. His chosen path was political, and in 1826 he became a Tory Member of Parliament. By 1828, he had become one of the leading political voices calling for an organized reaction to and improvement of the extraordinarily harsh working conditions and length of hours introduced into the country in the Industrial Revolution. He was lifting the curtain for the general public, displaying the reality behind the financial and economic triumphs produced by rapid industrialization. In particular, Cooper revealed, and demanded changes to, the employment of women and children in coal mines and the use of small children as chimney sweeps. He called for a ten-hour working day in factories, for care and compensation for those injured on the job, and for some sort of help for their dependants, and for the building of responsible and modern institutions for the mentally ill and the insane.

He campaigned tirelessly and gradually influenced the greater public and the political elite, leading to dramatic and widespread changes in the labour law and the use of children as workers. He wrote widely and spoke numerous times to pretty much any crowd that would listen.

Through all of his work, and especially when challenged and even physically threatened by vested interests with a great deal of money and prestige to lose if reform was allowed, he held to his Christian faith – it was the reason, the motivation, the power, behind what he did. He helped pass the *Mines Act* in 1842, and the *Ten Hours Act* five years later, known as Lord Ashley's Act. He became president of what was known as the Ragged Schools Union in 1843, and for forty years worked to provide free education for the poor children of London, and of the country's other large cities.[1]

On a private, personal level, and well away from the political field, he had model homes built on his own land, served as president of the British and Foreign Bible Society, and financed and personally worked for numerous missionary societies in London, Manchester, Liverpool, and elsewhere. Hand-in-hand with helping and reforming individual lives was the saving of individual souls. The cynical might look at this as something exploitative, but Shaftesbury and his followers never insisted on Christian belief for anybody they helped, but merely gave them the opportunity for such belief as and when they helped them. If it was rejected, so be it – the aid was not, could not, be withheld from those opposed to the inherent Christian message they were offering. Shaftesbury was also vastly ahead of his time in holding religious services in working-class theatres and downmarket music halls, for he always believed that Christianity was not to be the preserve of the middle class and the suburban.

He campaigned against systemic and personal racism and bigotry, stressing the dignity of Africans, and condemning anti-Semitism. He was also an extremely early advocate of Zionism, predating organized Jewish Zionism – Theodor Herzl would not publish *Der Judenstaat* until 1896. When Shaftesbury died in 1885, he had done more than most of his compatriots to change for the better the most powerful country on earth.

If Shaftesbury changed Britain, Dr. David Livingstone changed history. His tombstone reads,

> Brought by faithful hands over land and sea, David Livingstone: missionary, traveller, philanthropist. For 30 years his life was spent in an unwearied effort to evangelize the native races, to explore the undiscovered secrets, and to abolish the slave trade.

The language may seem a little archaic, but its message is bitingly contemporary. Racial justice, ethnic equality, and freedom. Two brief statements epitomize his life: "I will place no value on anything I have or may possess except in relation to the kingdom of Christ," and "If you have men who will only come if they know there is a good road, I don't want them. I want men who will come if there is no road at all."

Livingstone was born in 1813 in Blantyre, Scotland, and by the age of ten was working more than twelve hours a day in the local cotton mills. His family were intensely Protestant and encouraged within that Protestant tradition a love for learning, leading an exhausted Livingstone to read and study in the few hours he had to himself between work and sleep. He became fascinated with the East, and with China in particular, and eventually trained to become a medical missionary. The Opium War, however, changed Chinese attitudes toward foreigners, and to an extent foreign attitudes toward China, and as a result missionary work there became impossible. Instead, Livingstone looked to Africa, and by the 1840s was settled in the south of the continent. For the next thirty years he combined exploration, efforts to convert Africans to Christianity, and medical work with a struggle for racial dignity and a dedication to ending domestic slavery, and explaining – demanding – the acceptance of an independent Africa to Europe and North America. He was not always popular with other whites in Africa, and the Afrikaners of what would become South Africa in particular thought him a Christian extremist who was far too close to the natives. He was physically attacked, was denounced, and had his property stolen and destroyed and his home fire-bombed.[2]

It was something that never concerned him. Speaking to a meeting of students at Cambridge University, he said:

People talk of the sacrifice I have made in spending so much of my life in Africa. Can that be called a sacrifice which is simply paid back as a small part of a great debt owing to our God, which we can never repay? Is that a sacrifice which brings its own blest reward in healthful activity, the consciousness of doing good, peace of mind, and a bright hope of a glorious destiny hereafter? Away with the word in such a view and with such a thought! It is emphatically no sacrifice. Say rather it is a privilege. Anxiety, sickness, suffering, or danger now and then with a forgoing of the common conveniences and charities of this life, may make us pause and cause the spirit to waver and the soul to sink; but let this only be for a moment. All these are nothing when compared with the glory which shall be revealed in and for us. I never made a sacrifice.

Livingstone developed a natural bond with Africans, not based on some paternalistic attitude toward "noble savages," but by an empathy that he developed and never lost. It was love of Africa rather than white guilt that led him to fight so hard against slavery, and rather than merely working to expunge it, he realized that for slavery to be permanently eliminated it would have to be replaced by an alternative economic model and system. Livingstone was one of the first people to try to introduce capitalism in Africa, not to exploit, but to liberate and empower.

He was partly successful, less in transforming the African economy than in making Africa and the suffering and exploitation of its people common knowledge to a previously indifferent and ignorant world. What was known with a dismissive romanticism as the "dark" continent became within Livingstone's lifetime a central geopolitical issue in the moral conscience of the West. David Livingstone died in a village southeast of Lake Bangweulu on May 1, 1873, from malaria and dysentery, while kneeling in prayer. The British authorities wanted his body to be repatriated to Britain, but the tribe with whom Livingstone was living refused. Finally, they relented, but only after removing his heart, and placing a letter on his body stating, "You can have his body, but his heart belongs in Africa!"

For David Livingstone, the freedom of black Africa was paramount, but freedom and incarceration were also open wounds in Britain, and this was known especially well by the Christian social reformer Elizabeth Fry. Elizabeth Gurney was born in 1780, into an era when concepts of rehabilitation or restorative justice were not even within the lexicon of the judicial and prison system. Incarceration was supposed to be as brutal and relentless as possible, partly as a way of dissuading offenders from recommitting crimes in the future, but also as a form of state punishment of the individual. While rehabilitation and restorative justice both are now part of the prison system, it's the former that is emphasized over the latter, combined with a concerted attempt to reform character through education, the idea being that an offender who is offered alternatives to criminality will change, will not re-offend, and will not have to be re-incarcerated; the decline in recidivism will save the state money, make people and property safer, and be personally more compassionate. It doesn't always work, but it's far more successful than the organized brutality of the nineteenth century, and the changes owe an inestimable amount to the work of Christians like Elizabeth Fry and her friends.

At twenty, Gurney married Joseph Fry, a successful and wealthy tea merchant, and they would have eleven children. She had been raised a Christian, but underwent a deep and lasting conversion two years before her marriage. She described it: "I wish the state of enthusiasm I am now in may last, for today I FELT there is a God. I have been devotional and my mind has been led away from the follies that it is mostly wrapped up in." And, "Oh Lord, may I be directed what to do and what to leave undone." She left very little undone. She began by distributing food, clothing, and medicine to the poor in London, and with a group of other Christian women founded a nursing school known as the Sisters of Devonshire Square. In 1813, she changed direction and began to devote her considerable energies to the prison system, and in particular the women incarcerated in the city's notorious Newgate prison. One unfortunate inmate described it thus: "The mingled stench of disease and faeces and the cacophonous din of wailing and screeching in the maze of unventilated wards was unutterably horrifying." Fry saw this for herself and was devastated by the horribly overcrowded cells, the innocent who had been found guilty because they had no legal representation, those who had done nothing more than steal bread to feed their hunger spending decades in prison, and the legions of people sentenced to hang for non-violent crimes. "Does Capital punishment tend to the security of the people?" she asked rhetorically. "By no means. It hardens the hearts of men, and makes the loss of life appear light to them; it renders life insecure, inasmuch as the law holds out that Property is of greater value than life."

In the first half of the nineteenth century, mothers were imprisoned with their children, and both would be confined to tiny spaces, where they were expected to eat, sleep, defecate, and urinate. Crime and violence were rampant inside Newgate, and alcohol was stolen or bought from visitors and guards. This was a dangerous place, and no respecter of class or gender, yet Fry insisted on visiting on a daily basis, bringing in food and supplies, giving out Bibles and Gospel tracts, and spending hours speaking to and listening to women who had been ignored and rejected all their lives. In 1816, she started the Association for the Improvement of the Female Prisoners of Newgate, "to provide for the clothing, instruction, and employment of the women; to introduce them to a knowledge of the Holy Scriptures, and to form in them, as much as possible, those habits of sobriety, order, and industry, which may render them docile and peaceable while in prison, and respectable when they leave it." She expanded her commitment beyond personal involvement and individual cases, to an organized and national campaign to introduce systemic changes. She lobbied Members of Parliament and government ministers to separate men and women prisoners, to employ female guards to look after female prisoners, to distinguish between serious and less serious crimes, and to treat offenders as people who had committed crimes, rather than as the personifications of the crimes themselves.[3]

While she faced strong opposition from an entrenched prison system and the political structure around it, it was difficult for politicians who visited the prisons and spoke to the prisoners and former prisoners to argue against the proof of Fry's work. Women were being reformed, they were not re-offending, and fewer women were being incarcerated. The Newgate example began to influence other prisons, even those in other countries, and in 1823 the British Parliament passed the *Prison Reform Act*, initiating a wave of enlightened and progressive prison legislation. Fry went on to visit prison ships; she established half-way houses; and by the time she died in 1845, she had transformed the shape and nature of prisons, justice, and law and order. She wrote,

> Neither yield ye your members as instruments of unrighteousness unto sin but yield yourselves unto God, as those that are alive from the dead, and your members as instruments of righteousness unto God. . . . Make you perfect in every good work to do his will, working in you that which is well pleasing in his sight, through Jesus Christ; to whom be glory for ever and ever.

Such words might also characterize the life of Florence Nightingale, who was born in 1820 in Florence, Italy, to a prosperous English family. She was well-educated, but given few opportunities as a woman to fulfil her academic potential. When she was just sixteen, she had a conversion experience and felt that God was calling her to do something extraordinary, even revolutionary, with her life. It was a meeting with Lord

Shaftesbury that channelled these new energies into the idea of social reform. On the one hand was Shaftesbury's advice and Nightingale's own Christian commitment, and on the other was the competing pressure from her family encouraging her to settle down, marry, and start a family. The great catalyst in her decision-making was her caring for her ill grandmother, whom she looked after with a compassion and professionalism seldom seen in full-time nurses. "So never lose an opportunity of urging a practical beginning, however small," she said, "for it is wonderful how often in such matters the mustard-seed germinates and roots itself."

Nightingale decided that her vocation was to become a hospital nurse, but her parents forbade it. Not surprising, in that nurses in the early nineteenth century were not held in high esteem and were regarded as the servants of servants, and even "women of easy virtue." The more she was insulted and abused, the more determined she became. She toured Europe, investigating medical conditions and studying the nursing profession, and then in 1853, in spite of her parents' protests, became superintendant of a hospital for "sick gentlewomen." Opportunity came in blood-soaked disaster in 1854 in the form of Britain's war, alongside France, Turkey, and Piedmont in the Crimea against the Russian empire. Because her family knew Britain's minister of war, Sidney Herbert, Nightingale was able to lead a team of thirty-eight nurses to Scutari in Turkey, and begin to work with wounded soldiers living in deplorable conditions. Her opinion: "No man, not even a doctor, ever gives any other definition of what a nurse should be than this – 'devoted and obedient.' This definition would do just as well for a porter. It might even do for a horse. It would not do for a policeman." Armed with this spirit, she set out to help men who were left to rot and die in filthy beds, with an open sewer underneath the hospital, stinking out the entire place, and making meaningful medical care virtually impossible. She recorded at the time:

> What the horrors of war are, no one can imagine. . . . They are not wounds and blood and fever, spotted and low, or dysentery, chronic and acute, cold and heat and famine. They are intoxication, drunken brutality, demoralization and disorder on the part of the inferior . . . jealousies, meanness, indifference, selfish brutality on the part of the superior.[4]

After the battle of Balaclava, matters became even worse. It was a horribly costly and ultimately pointless encounter, and men with smashed limbs and ripped stomachs limped back to their lines desperate for help. The nurses were now essential, dealing with wounds, cleaning the blood and vomit from the floors, easing the pain, and holding brave, broken men as they died. It was at this time that Florence Nightingale was given the nickname "The Lady with the Lamp," due to her constant wandering around the hospital late at night to make sure that the men were cared for, fed, and kept clean, and the hospital properly heated. By now her reputation had spread far beyond the Crimea, and in 1855 Queen Victoria wrote to her to give her thanks. More importantly, because of the newspaper coverage of Nightingale and her nurses, other hospitals were forced to follow this new pattern of care, compassion, and cleanliness. A Royal Commission on hospitals and medical care was established, and most of its recommendations eventually implemented. In 1860, the Nightingale School of Nursing was founded, followed by another Royal Commission on Indian health care, and a series of nursing manuals and guides written by Nightingale being given to every new hospital and providing the foundation for nursing care. Florence Nightingale died in 1910, leaving a world eternally changed for the better.

Wellesley C. Bailey was another Christian whose faith propelled him into caring for the needy and the marginalized, and establishing a new norm for the care of some of the most despised and feared in ancient and modern society: lepers. So rejected were these men and women who suffered from leprosy that the word even became a metaphor for the social outcast. Not so for Bailey.

He was born in Ireland in 1846 and became a Christian as a young man. After making a substantial amount of money in Australia, he decided to travel in India. He was shocked by the general poverty and deprivation, but in particular by the leper colony he toured. There was relatively little that could be done for sufferers in the nineteenth century, and for millennia the solution had been to isolate these poor souls from society, making them live in groups with other lepers, and even ring bells if they travelled, which they rarely did, so that healthy people could be warned of their approach and avoid them. Bailey sold some of his possessions and began to spend increasingly long periods of time with the lepers, putting himself at medical risk, and naturally making him a voluntary social outcast to many. He supplied them with food, drink, and clothes, built houses for them and paid for doctors to visit.

He also shared the Gospels with them and worked to convert them to Christianity, sometimes personally baptizing them. Which is where, inevitably, he is criticized by modern writers, who accuse him of being someone who exploited the sick and lonely to spread his religious beliefs. It was, runs the condemnation, a form of theological and ideological imperial-ism. It's significant that this was not an accusation made at the time, or by the lepers themselves. The attack is based on an artificial construct: Bailey, like so many Christian social reform-ers, was not using social work to spread Christianity, but was inspired by Christianity to spread social work. Neither he nor any of the Christian activists mentioned in this book even con-templated refusing or withdrawing aid and help to those who rejected the Christian message, nor were they competing with non-Christian reformers or secularists who were trying to do similar work. What we see repeatedly is that Christians were the only people trying to change the situation, which can only be considered a coincidence by people who are far more credu-lous and gullible than those who believe in God and miracles.

Bailey returned to Ireland in 1873 and gave lectures and wrote articles in the British and Irish press about his experiences in India. He raised money, campaigned, and raised awareness about a community ignored for generations. Two years later he sailed back to India and established a new, model asylum for lepers at Chamba, then another in Burma in 1889, followed by similar institutions in South Africa, Japan, Korea, and elsewhere. He died in 1937, aged ninety-one, and had effectively changed the way lepers and leprosy were perceived and understood.

Beyond the literal lepers were the figurative outsiders, espe-cially the poor, the young, and the uneducated. It was to this group that Georg Muller devoted his life. He wrote,

> God's plan is there shall be none of self and all of Christ. . . .
> The very people who are doing the most for God in saving
> souls, in mission work, in the care of orphans, are those who

are working on short supplies of strength, of money, of talents, of advantages, and are kept in a position of living by faith and taking from God, day by day both physical and spiritual supplies. This is the way God succeeds and gains conquests over His own people, and over the unbelief of those who look on His providences.

Muller was born in 1805 in Prussia and attended school and university in Germany, where he tried desperately hard not to allow work and sacrifice interfere with his fun and self-indulgence. He was a playboy. But as a young man he underwent a Christian conversion, and from the age of twenty devoted himself to charity work and religious study. In 1829, he accepted a position with the London Society for Promoting Christianity among the Jews, but in spite of learning Hebrew and studying Jewish culture, he couldn't settle in the position; the same was true when he was made minister of a small church, and then when he became a missionary in Iran. There was a restlessness about him, a nervous energy and an enormous urge to do good, but he couldn't find a target and a purpose for it all. Until he moved to Bristol, in the west of England, and encountered the utter destitution of children who were orphaned, exploited by family members, used as workers or even exchanged as sex objects on the street. The entire concept we have today of children and their role and place in society was utterly alien to Europe in the first half of the nineteenth century. Orphans and street children in particular were viewed as being products of sinful and fallen behaviour, and somehow responsible for their own situations. They were seen as small, troubled adults, not as innocent, vulnerable children. It was a belief that Muller completely rejected, and in 1836 he and his wife offered their home as a sanctuary for 30 girls. This was soon followed by the opening of a further three houses, with 130 children in care, and then in 1845 a new, purpose-built house to cater to up to 300 children.

By now, Muller's reputation and that of his work was spreading throughout the country, and parents unable to look after their children were sending them to the "Muller houses." By 1870, there were five more homes, with almost 1,800 children cared for, fed, and given a safety and security that most of them had never known before. As the success of the houses became known, other Christians formed support societies to raise money, and to donate food and clothes. Muller made a point of not explicitly asking for donations, but millions of dollars would eventually be given to him and his work.

Each day at the houses was heavily structured, beginning with prayer and Bible-reading after breakfast, an emphasis on basic reading and writing skills, and a constant reminder that each child was dignified and worthy of respect not only as a child, but as a child of God. It's easy to mock such a concept today, but for these boys and girls it was a self-image that was unique and transformed their lives. Muller invited, even demanded, that independent school inspectors come into his homes to guarantee that the children were being well taken care of, and was scrupulous in his sense of transparency. When the children graduated from the homes, they were given their own Bible, a trunk with two sets of clothes, and introductions to various Christian employers who Muller was sure would treat them well and give them a trade. Over the years, he would change, often save, the lives of tens of thousands of children directly, and indirectly change Victorian society by showing the innate worth of these otherwise anonymous, ignored young people.

———

Muller was just one of so many Christians inspired to reshape the world in a Godly image, who had read the words of the great evangelist John Wesley: "Do all the good you can, By all the means you can, In all the ways you can, In all the places you can, At all the times you can, To all the people you can, As long as ever you can"; "Catch on fire with enthusiasm and people will come for miles to watch you burn"; and "Beware you be not swallowed up in books! An ounce of love is worth a pound of knowledge."

Wesley was born in Lincolnshire in the English Midlands in 1703, the son of an Anglican minister. He was educated at Charterhouse school in London, and then at Christchurch College Oxford. It was on his return to Oxford, after being ordained a deacon in the Church of England, that he became president of what was known as the Oxford Holy Club. This group of devoted Christians had been founded by John's brother Charles and was composed of young men who dedicated their lives to serving God and performing good works. They were regularly ridiculed by other Oxford students and accused of extremism. The attacks encouraged rather than dissuaded them, and as they mingled the work of visiting prisoners in the local jail and organizing kitchens to feed the poor with intense, often silent prayer, they managed to change the minds of a number of students who had previously rejected Christianity. Those who remained unconvinced would shout at them through their room windows and sing the rhyme,

By rule they eat, by rule they drink,
By rule do all things but think.
Accuse the priests of loose behaviour.
To get more in the laymen's favour.

Method alone must guide 'em all,
When themselves "Methodists" they call.

Such was the beginning of the Methodist Church.

In fact, Wesley remained a member of the Church of England all his life, and it was only after his death that a new, separate denomination emerged, that itself gave rise to other churches in the next century. He emphasized the need for personal holiness, a constant sense of conversion, and the vital place in Christian life for works and deeds. It was why the anti-slavery movement was so soaked in Wesleyan Christianity, and it is no exaggeration to say that without it, abolition in Britain would have taken far longer to achieve. It is estimated that Wesley rode more than 250,000 miles on horseback to preach, visit the needy, and spread the word of social progress and Christian truth. He also gave away a fortune in charity. In a single year, for example, in which he earned the modern equivalent of $1.4 million, Wesley kept a mere 2 percent for himself to live on, and gave the other 98 percent to deserving causes. He is estimated to have earned more than $30 million in his life in today's money, but on his death in 1791 he had only a handful of coins and a few silver spoons.[5]

Beyond his personal piety and generosity, however, was the influence he and his followers had on transforming British, and by extension North American, society. He proudly told people that "there is no holiness but social holiness!" and as early as his student days studied basic medicine and first aid in his spare time. This, he said, was a good personal example, but to change the condition of the mass of people, society had to change its collective mind and regard people not as a mass but as a group of individual souls. It is impossible to overestimate the influence this approach had on Britain in particular, and it's often been said that the Labour Party, which has governed the country for decades since the 1920s, owed far more to Methodism than to Marx. In other words, it was Wesleyan Christianity rather than socialism that was the major impetus behind the creation of a welfare system, universal health care, old age pensions, and so on. It is similarly argued that the reason the revolutionary violence of Europe in the 1790s and 1840s was not replicated in Britain was due to the reforming and sobering influence of the Methodist movement. But Methodism also emphasized self-reliance. So Methodists helped people find jobs and establish homes, but also campaigned against unfair rates of interest – "rescuing them (the poor) from lenders demanding extortionate interest that would have compounded their distress." Even as recently as the late twentieth century, the struggle against South African apartheid was heavily influenced by British and African Methodism, and the racial justice imperative of the various churches flavoured by the social gospel.

But if one man epitomized that racial struggle and fundamentally altered the relationship between black and white, and powerful and powerless, it was Martin Luther King. A Christian? Very much so. "To be a Christian without prayer," he said, "is no more possible than to be alive without breathing," and

But though I was initially disappointed at being categorized as an extremist, as I continued to think about the matter I gradually gained a measure of satisfaction from the label. Was not Jesus an extremist for love: "Love your enemies, bless them that curse you, do good to them that hate you, and pray for them which despitefully use you, and persecute you."

Then, later,

In that dramatic scene on Calvary's hill three men were crucified. We must never forget that all three were crucified for the same crime – the crime of extremism. Two were extremists for immorality, and thus fell below their environment. The other, Jesus Christ, was an extremist for love, truth and goodness, and thereby rose above his environment. Perhaps the South, the nation and the world are in dire need of creative extremists.

He was born Michael Luther King in January 1929, but later changed his name to Martin. His grandfather had been the minister at Ebenezer Baptist Church in Atlanta, Georgia, followed by his father, and Martin was co-pastor from 1960. Like most black Americans in the South, he attended segregated schools, and then went to Morehouse College, an all-black university in Atlanta. From there, after graduation, he attended Crozer Theological Seminary, a mixed college in Pennsylvania, and was elected president of his mostly white class. From there, with his degree in Divinity, he went on to Boston University, gaining his doctorate in 1955. It was in Boston that he met his wife, Coretta, and they would go on to have four children. It was in 1954, when he became the pastor of the Dexter Avenue Baptist Church in Montgomery, Alabama, while also being a member of the executive committee of the NAACP (National Association for the Advancement of Colored People) that he became acutely political.

After half a century of books, movies, documentaries, and education, it's tempting to believe that the change from systemic racism to assumed racial equality in the United States was inevitable and almost unavoidable, but in the 1950s this was far from the case. Change would probably have happened in some form at some point, but not without colossal violence, and leading to a nation more divided than we can perhaps imagine. Speaking out against discrimination in the Deep South was dangerous and difficult, and not even supported by all of the black community. As humiliating as segregation, lack of rights, and abuse may have been, there were still people in all areas of life who preferred to look the other way for any number of reasons. In December 1955, Martin Luther King initiated and led the massive bus boycott that would last for more than a year, leading to the country's Supreme Court ruling that such segregation was unconstitutional. It was a seminal moment in American history, and in the greater history of race and power. A candle had been lit that could not and would not now be extinguished. King's enemies knew this as well as he did, which is why they fire-bombed his home, tried to kill him, physically attacked his supporters, and did all in their power to silence the figurehead of racial liberation. King personified the black struggle to white America, and while he would never win over the extremists, his Christian commitment to non-violence convinced millions that change was long overdue.

In 1957, he became president of the Southern Christian Leadership Conference, an organization directly inspired by Christian principles, designed to form new, young leaders for the civil rights movement. Between 1957 and 1968, the preacher from Atlanta and Alabama became one of the most famous and visible figures in the world. He travelled almost seven million miles, wrote books and articles, spoke thousands of times, and led protests in towns and cities all across the United States. He was arrested, beaten, and insulted. He was promised death, but responded that while he walked with God he would not fear. *Time* magazine named him Man of the Year, and he became the youngest man to ever win the Nobel Peace Prize.

In 1963 in Washington, this leader made a speech that is one of the most significant, iconic, and influential of modern times. It was longer than many people today realize, and drenched in the powerful prose and poetry of the Christian tradition. It culminated with

> I have a dream today. I have a dream that one day every valley shall be exalted, every hill and mountain shall be made low, the rough places will be made plain, and the crooked places will be made straight, and the glory of the Lord shall be revealed, and all flesh shall see it together. This is our hope. This is the faith that I go back to the South with.

On April 4, 1968, Martin Luther King was assassinated while on the balcony of his hotel in Memphis, Tennessee, and the country has yet to see his like again. A martyr for his race, a martyr for his country, a martyr for justice, and a martyr for – and this he would have screamed from every podium – Christ and the Christian faith. And this is something that must not be, cannot be, separated from the very fabric and being of the people mentioned here, and the plethora of other Christians trying so hard, and often making the ultimate sacrifice, to make the world a better place. They do so not in spite of, but because of, their beliefs. Without Christianity they are empty vessels, incapable of achieving anything; not my words, but theirs.

IX

CHRISTIANS ARE OBSESSED WITH ABORTION

THIS IS AN ATTACK CHRISTIANS HEAR ALL THE TIME, to the point where it actually leads some believers to abandon their opposition to abortion because they fear it will detract from their ability to speak to people about Christianity. This is not only tragic for the unborn, but terribly short-sighted – if a Christian does not stand firm for the weakest in our society, what sort of a Christian are they? Christians are not obsessed with abortion, but they do care passionately about human life. The attack also implies, either directly or indirectly, that abortion is the only political, moral, and sociological subject that Christians care about, which is as false as it is malicious. But it's important to outline why Christians are so vocal about the abortion issue, and so often the only people who are vocal about the issue. Actually, this should come as no surprise, for throughout history Christians have led campaigns dealing with various social catastrophes and evils, and have often been largely alone. This was the case, as we have seen, with the fight against slavery, the campaign against child labour, and so on. It's not that slavery, child labour, or abortion are specifically Christian issues, but that Christians are more attuned to notions of good and evil, right and wrong, and thus more likely and willing to speak out. This statement, of course, will provoke anti-Christians to apoplexy, but Christians are also in tune with those suffering from apoplexy, and are more than happy to help.

The actual arguments against abortion are partly Biblical – Psalm 139 has this:

> For you created my inmost being; you knit me together in my mother's womb. I praise you because I am fearfully and wonderfully made; your works are wonderful, I know that full well. My frame was not hidden from you when I was made in the secret place. When I was woven together in the depths of the earth, your eyes saw my unformed body. All the days ordained for me were written in your book before one of them came to be.

Job has "Did not he who made me in the womb make them? Did not the same one form us both within our mothers?" and Jeremiah, "Before I formed you in the womb I knew you, before you were born I set you apart; I appointed you as a prophet to the nations." But the Christian stance on the issue is at heart a position based on the moral and the logical, and an inevitable consequence of an understanding of science and human rights. All rights are important, but the most inalienable and the most fundamental is the right to life. In fact, no right has any meaning unless it is underpinned by the most natural and essential right and that is, of course, the right to be allowed to be born.[1]

The scientific arguments first, because whenever Christians mention abortion, they are accused of bringing religion into politics, when in fact they are bringing rational thought and scientific fact into politics. What we know, and what has nothing to do with theology or belief, is that at the moment of conception, a male sperm unites with a female ovum to fertilize it, and the single-celled organism formed is called a zygote, an intricate and sophisticated repository of biological information of both parents. Fertilization occurs in the Fallopian tube and shortly afterwards cells move to the uterine wall of the womb. Within the next twenty-four to forty-eight hours, the tiny zygote multiplies at an extraordinary rate and becomes what is called a blastocyst, containing one hundred cells. This is called the embryo and will be until the eighth week of development. From the eighth week until birth, the word fetus is used. One month after conception, the eyes, ears, and respiratory stem are developing, and three weeks later the baby is sucking its thumb. A week later, the heart can be felt beating, and the following week the baby can grip and bend its fingers. Eleven weeks after conception there is steady breathing, and then the baby will be able to swallow the amniotic fluid. Around two weeks after this, around fourteen weeks from conception, the baby can taste, and between sixteen and twenty weeks the baby can hear, including hearing its mother's heartbeat. At twenty-three weeks after conception the baby is sleeping regularly, and six months after conception the baby's sweat glands are functioning. The following month the baby kicks, stretches, performs somer-saults. From this point on there is considerable weight gain, and at around nine months the baby is born and, suddenly, has a right to life, liberty, education, and the right to free speech, health care, assembly, and whatever else. It all seems rather arbitrary that these secondary rights are suddenly given to a person who up until that point had no right under law to be born and to not be killed. No religion here, nothing of the supernatural, just Christians articulating scientific truth.[2]

And remember, as science and medicine advances, we will be able to preserve the lives of more and more early-term babies at earlier and earlier periods in their development. They will be able to survive outside of the womb at a very young age. Does this still mean that abortion is based on the point of independent, viable life? Not that it seems to matter very much even now, because there are ghoulish cases where babies have survived abortion and been left to die. In other such cases, nurses have intervened to save the life of the baby, which raises any number of questions that in a saner scientific and ethical environment would never have to be asked.

At the earliest point, at conception, a child has a unique DNA and genomic character and is already unlike anyone who has been conceived or born before or anyone who will be conceived or born afterwards. It is a distinct human life and like all human life in a civilized society should have a right to exist. Yet the last twenty years have seen a curious twisting of the debate around the abortion issue and a monumentally successful campaign to marginalize pro-life opinion, especially when that pro-life opinion is held by Christians. Politicians at every level and in almost every country are told that to even discuss the policy would lose them votes – though polls repeatedly show people at best as being divided on the subject – and opponents of abortion, whatever their views on other issues, are portrayed as single-issue extremists. This has made an informed, respectful discussion of the issue extremely difficult because the mere mention of abortion is enough to make many people in politics, media, and public life turn away as if their lives were threatened. Actually it's not their lives but the lives of unborn children that are in danger.[3]

Beyond the scientific, there are numerous arguments against abortion, but it's important to remember that none of them are in any way specifically Christian, but all of them rational, scientific, and ethical. When we hear of the issue of choice, and of course that Christians are anti-choice or against choice, it's essential to know what we mean by the word. By implication and assumption, choice is something entirely positive and is a product of, or in itself produces, freedom. On a serious level, the right and freedom to choose how to vote, what religion to practise, or what to read, believe, and say, are precious aspects of a civilized society. On a less important level, but still good and positive, is the choice of clothes, food, or even sports team or television show. So, choice is good, and it's good to support choice. So, of course, being against choice makes you a bad person, someone on the wrong side of history. But all sorts of choices are negative and harmful, and for them we never use the word choice. The choice to kill, rape, hurt and harm, steal, and libel are not considered choices but crimes. Even the choice to lie, betray, envy, or gossip may not be illegal, but nobody choosing them is thought to be acting properly and admirably. So the choice to abort, to kill an unborn baby, to end the life of your child simply because you have the power to do so, for whatever reason, is not really a choice in any meaningful sense, but an action currently supported by law and custom, not in any way connected with what we would otherwise define as choice.[4]

Then we have the argument that is often made by people who want to please all camps around this position. They say that they do not approve of abortion themselves and would never have an abortion, but would not stop someone else from having an abortion. The problem is, it just makes no sense. It's probably why it's so often used by politicians. This is not difficult stuff and is actually quite simple, if uncomfortable. If abortion is not the taking of a life it is always permissible, and we should not make laws against it, and we should not oppose it. But if it is the taking of a life it is never permissible, it is always wrong, and we should always oppose it. And it is, as we have seen, a human life, and the reason to be opposed to it is that it is truly the killing of an innocent human being; as this is so, one does not have the option of personally not wanting to kill while enabling and allowing others to do so. The person who buys the gun for the killer is also guilty; the person who does nothing to stop the shooter is also guilty; even the person who just doesn't care about the shooting crime is also morally guilty. If it's wrong, it's wrong. This is not an ethically neutral act, even if so many people pretend it to be so because they fear social abuse or political defeat if they take a stand.

Nor is it about what a woman can or cannot do with her body. Obviously in any progressive society a woman should have, and generally has, the choice to do whatever she wants with a tuft of hair or an appendix, and certainly with her own body as long as the act does not harm others. But does she have the right to tamper with or kill a distinct person within her? The unborn child generally cannot survive outside of the womb, but then a fully developed newborn child, or for that matter an injured or sick adult, will die quickly if left without care. A person hit by a car will often die unless we help them, but we would think little of someone who did not help them, and who walked on past the smashed victim of a car accident. Size is the most obvious difference between an unborn child and a fully developed baby or a teenager or an adult, but this is a facile and cosmetic observation, and says far more about us than it does about the baby in question. In fact, after three months of growth, there is no new major development in an unborn baby, and at nine months the unborn child may be more mature than it was, but then a five-year-old is more mature than a two-year-old, and a teenager more mature than a ten-year-old. We have been influenced by media and by social propaganda to think otherwise, but we know instinctively that the unborn baby is a child, witnessed for example by how we would react if we saw an obviously pregnant woman smoking or drinking. We've been programmed to think differently if we see a pregnant woman opting to end the life of her powerless child. If a heavily pregnant woman walked into a bar and began to drink, many people would be outraged and tell her to stop. We've become morally schizophrenic and ethically desensitized, and much of the reluctance to consider the issue is precisely because when people do study abortion beyond the hyperbole of the mistakenly and misleadingly named pro-choice argument they become so terribly disturbed and distressed. So they'd rather be ignorant than challenged, and the Christians who push them on the abortion issue make them feel especially uneasy.[5]

The arguments for abortion have been heard numerous times, especially in a North American and European media that is so often devoted to the abortion cause, sometimes to a degree where journalists will ignore enormously attended pro-life events and distort the pro-life message. It is staggering how often a hysterical opponent of abortion is found to articulate the argument against abortion on mainstream media, while numerous intelligent, gentle, informed experts are still waiting for their chance. While those in the pro-life movement are regularly accused of obsession, it seems to be their opponents who are the truly committed, never wasting an opportunity to promote their position and to dismiss pro-life arguments. How many detective dramas have we seen, for example, where abortion doctors are killed? Such a violent action is never justified and is, thankfully and contrary to what some would have us believe, incredibly rare. Then again, compared to the millions of children aborted in recent years, an isolated assault on an abortion doctor does rather pale in comparison. So, frankly, do the arguments in favour of abortion when they're carefully considered. We've heard them time and time again, and they are no more compelling on the fiftieth or hundredth performance.

How about abortion, runs one of the most common debating points, in cases of rape and incest? The truth, rather than the false emotionalism, is that these tragedies provide less than a fraction of one per cent of the reasons for abortion and they are mentioned by abortion advocates simply to make pro-lifers appear extreme – those callous pro-life advocates don't care about rape victims or young girls forced into sex by a father. No Christian who has argued for the unborn in a debate has escaped this one, and it's usually delivered in portentous tones, as if the statement itself was the final argument on the entire issue. As much as it's a horrible scenario, and one to be taken seriously and treated with the utmost sympathy and compassion, it must not be allowed to sway or win an argument. We should ask if those who support abortion in these rare and grotesque cases would be prepared to oppose abortion when rape and incest are not the causes of pregnancy. In almost every case it's a rhetorical question; the incest and rape approach tends to have far more to do with defeating a pro-lifer than in helping a poor victim of rape or incest. Christians believe that life is sacred and that while love, empathy, and understanding are essential, we cannot punish one crime by committing another. A rapist is a criminal, his child is not. Having said all this, however, there are also people who are the children of rapists. In other words, men and women whose mothers were raped and who are alive because those women refused to have an abortion, even though they had suffered so much. Try looking such a person in the eye, and explaining how it would have been a better thing if they had never been born.

But surely if abortion is not legal and readily available, the argument continues, there will be countless deaths in back-street abortions. This is an extremely disingenuous argument, because as so-called backstreet abortions only occurred because abortion was illegal, we cannot know how many they were. They were, by their nature, illegal, and thus there were no records: criminals do not keep detailed accounts of their offences. There is no doubt that back-street abortions occurred, that women were treated terribly and were exploited and sometimes died. We know for a fact, though, that women die in legal, often publicly funded front-street abortions and that abortion is often encouraged either indirectly by the culture or directly by the abortion industry, which is not, as some would have us believe, purely altruistic, interested only in women's health and indifferent to profit. The problem is not where the abortion takes place, but that it takes place anywhere at all. When it does, a baby is killed. Of course, there were illegal abortions, and of course there would be illegal abortions again, if ever abortion was made an offence, but that reflects the nature of crime and law-breaking, not whether abortion is right or wrong. Murder and theft are illegal, but they still occur; imagine how many murders and how much stealing there would be, if we suddenly made them legal.

Another regular attack is based on the notion that only women have a right to comment on this issue. For such a serious subject, one about life and death, this is painfully fatuous. Men are fathers, men are taxpayers, men are citizens, and men are also certainly abortionists. Actually most abortionists are men, and most of the people who profit from the abortion industry are men. Men are also frequently responsible for abortions, in that they do not fulfil their roles as fathers, they abandon vulnerable women who are pregnant, and they bring pressure to bear on women whom they have made pregnant because they do not want the responsibilities of fatherhood. Surely it is the quality of the argument rather than the gender of the individual making the argument that should inform our position. Nor do those women who argue that men should not comment about abortion even mean this; what they mean is that men who oppose abortion should not comment about the issue, but then again they usually believe that no person, male or female, should speak out against abortion. At a philosophical level, the laws of a state are not formed only by the people whom they directly affect, but by the full state, represented and led by the government and the judiciary for the good and protection of all people, whatever their gender, race, religion, or background.

Gender bias does, however, play a direct and dire part in the abortion phenomenon, in that it leads to far more baby girls being aborted than baby boys. In the past twenty tears in particular, modern technology has met with archaic gender preferences and religious misogyny (non-Christian religious misogyny, by the way) and in parts of the Third World in particular, and in diaspora communities in Europe and North America, women are aborting babies if they are female and keeping them if they're male. It's rather a bitter paradox for feminist ideology, yet if the unborn child is genuinely nothing more than tissue with no rights, this should not be an issue. But it is an issue for many people who are otherwise vehemently pro-abortion, meaning that they've been living something of an ideological and political lie. They may argue that the specific killing of unborn little girls is morally irrelevant, but viscerally they react badly to it because they know it is wrong. They know they are girls, and girls being killed purely because of their sex. I have seen the almost physical pain of pro-choice feminists when confronted with the reality of gender-based abortion. On the one hand, they feel compelled to defend abortion, on the other they cringe at the idea that babies are aborted solely because they are female.

It is not only little girls who are chosen for selected death however. While the unborn in general are supremely vulnerable, the handicapped or disabled unborn are even more so. We claim to be living in an enlightened age, and one that is more progressive and tolerant than at any time in the past, and certainly more diverse and kind than the Christian-based societies of old that we so like to use as examples of how we have evolved and become more broad-minded and pluralistic. One of the great boasts is that we provide facilities for handicapped people, and we congratulate ourselves on how we care for them and try to make their lives easier. Yet simultaneously, we allow or even encourage abortion that now deliberately targets those whose handicap can be detected in the womb. Once again, as science has progressed, it has been exploited to commit wrong rather than to extend right. Children with Down Syndrome are being aborted at a terrifying rate, and there may well come a time when we hardly ever see such people in society, and where few if any children will even know what a Down Syndrome person looked like. On the one hand, we tell people with physical and mental challenges that they are equal and that everybody has equal worth, but at the same time we offer, allow, and sometimes encourage – it is standard for a doctor to inform a mother if an unborn baby has what is known as a "defect" and offer the grand euphemism of an "alternative to birth" – the removal of babies who may grow up looking a little different from the rest of the population. Think for a moment about the deliberate creation of a society where one group of people have been expunged, or eliminated, merely for being who and what they are and what they look like. They have done nothing wrong and may well be gentler, kinder, and less aggressive and cruel than most other people, but the decision has still been taken to prevent them from ever being born. They will be removed.

Similar arguments apply to embryonic stem-cell research, and Christianity's resistance to it. As we saw elsewhere in this book in the science chapter, Christianity has been the great promoter of science and scientific progress, and Christians are not at all opposed to stem-cell research, but are opposed to the taking of cells from unborn children who cannot, obviously, give their permission. The distinction is extremely important, and one that is either unknown or deliberately ignored by anti-Christians. Stem cells can be taken from all sorts of sources: from umbilical cords, from the placenta, from amniotic fluid, from adult tissues and organs such as bone marrow, fat from liposuction, and even from regions of the nose. Difficult though it might be to believe, stem cells can be taken from cadavers up to twenty hours after death. There are, in fact, four different types of stem cell: embryonic stem cells, embryonic germ cells, umbilical cord stem cells, and adult stem cells. In that germ cells can be obtained from miscarriages that do not involve an abortion, what becomes obvious to anybody prepared to look properly at this subject is that Christians only oppose one of the three forms of stem-cell research, which may be surprising to some in the media that have created the impression that if it were not for Christianity's opposition to stem-cell research, cures for any number of terrible diseases and illnesses would be found almost overnight. Although enormous progress has been made with stem-cell research, there is not a case of a single person being cured through the use of embryonic cells, partly because adult stem cells are obviously part of an adult body, whereas embryonic stem cells are not. If only this was more widely known and more widely discussed when the issue of stem-cell research is debated.

What this entire argument is really about, however, is whether it is morally acceptable to use an aborted child for medical research, or whether we should be allowed to create with the use of exploitative science some sort of clone – and remember that the creation of a cloned embryo for the purpose of harvesting cells is still the initiation of life for the sole purpose of using that life, even for noble purposes. Yet some argue that as abortions already take place – and in horribly large numbers – it is tragic and wasteful to merely discard these embryos when, whether we object to abortion or not, they could be used for a specific medical purpose and to help humanity. It's true that these babies may be dead, but to humiliate and abuse them even after death, and then to mutilate their tiny bodies, is an extra insult to a unique human being. More than this, it is also likely to encourage further abortions in poor countries, with women being bribed to conceive and then abort so as to help ill and sick people in the developed, wealthy world. It's tragic but true that medical science does not always allow itself to be determined by greater ethics, an example being the medical experiments conducted by the Nazis in the 1940s and some of the results obtained by the use of concentration camp inmates and political prisoners. Modern science has come to a consensus that any findings thus gathered cannot be used and very few people would disagree with this. The human body possesses an innate and natural dignity and even in death we cannot use a human body for whatever purpose we want without prior consent. Science is neither moral nor immoral, but exists in itself and to a large extent for itself. It is for us to make sure that it is used for good. Christianity rejects the notion of a human hierarchy, whether it is based on race, gender, ability, or age. Black, white, male, female, handicapped or able-bodied, unborn, middle-aged, old, dying, or in the prime of life. No person should have immoral authority over another merely because they have the power advantage through size, wealth, privilege, or race. It seems an eminently humanistic proposal, but when Christians articulate it they are accused of allowing religion to interfere in politics. Yes, they are, and thank God for it.

We're also told that abortion is a good thing because the world is already overpopulated and will be even more so in the future. Interestingly enough, we don't hear this claim in the developing world, in Africa and Asia, but increasingly and aggressively in the wealthy world, in western Europe and North America. The truth, though, is that the world is not overpopulated, but that the wealthy, developed world tends to be extremely greedy. Africa is a prime example of a continent treated badly and exploited, politically and economically, by the very people now complaining that Africans have too many children. One painful, poignant example of this concerns the African wild-growing grass called *Hoodia gordonii*. Africans have realized over the years that if they sucked and chewed the grass, the pains associated with hunger and starvation were not quite so bad. When this was discovered by Westerners, they imported *Hoodia gordonii* to the United States, to be turned into capsule form and sold to overweight people to help them in their efforts to diet. When Christians point out the double standard of all this, and how we should be far more concerned about African starvation than about Western obesity, and how reducing the African population is no solution to anything, they are condemned for being, once again, obsessed with abortion.[6] Humans in fact actually occupy around 3 per cent of the earth's land surface. To put that in perspective, if twelve hundred square feet was given to every person in the world they would still all fit into an area the size of Texas – not sure how the people of Texas would react to this. The other vital factor is that while the world's population is increasing, the world's *rate of population growth* is declining. United Nations figures reveal that the 79 countries that make up 40 percent of the world's population now have fertility rates too low to prevent population decline. The fertility rate in Asia fell from 2.4 between 1960 and 1965 to 1.5 between 1990 and 1995. In Latin America and the Caribbean for the same dates, the rates fell from 2.75 to 1.70. Europe, of course, is rapidly losing its population altogether – the rate was 0.16 between 1990 and 1995, which really means zero. What Westerners are really saying is that there are too many people around who do not look like us.[7]

This defence of the unborn and defence of larger families in the Third World sometimes leads Christians into conflict with environmentalism, which itself has taken on a quasi-religious fervour. This is one of the reasons why Christians should be extremely careful when embracing fashionable ecological ideals and embracing the green agenda. What is green is not always good, and certainly not always Christian. Environmentalists worry that a larger population will damage the planet and have disastrous effects on the planet's ecological system. Remember, many if not most of the especially lovely parts of the world with the greatest environmental quality are in densely populated countries. Rain forests, for example, are not disappearing because of overpopulation, but because of Western demand for what is in the rainforests. In Brazil, where some of the major damage is occurring, the population per square mile is far less than half the world average. As for air and water pollution, some of the most egregious cases of damage and poor quality have been in countries such as Poland, Russia, and China, where population growth is extremely low. The Food and Agriculture Organization of the United Nations estimates that food surpluses are close to 50 per cent in the developed world and around 17 per cent in the developing world – hardly proof that people starve because of too little food. Food supplies have doubled in the last fifty years and farmers currently work on half the world's arable land. The food is there, if it is distributed fairly and competently. The Ethiopian famine in 1984 and 1985 is a horrendous case not of people dying due to lack of food, but of a corrupt government stealing food from farmers and businessmen and selling it to buy arms. It was socialism and not overpopulation that led to the terrible suffering. Africa in fact has one-fifth the population density of Europe, and Taiwan, with five times the population density of mainland China, produces much more per capita than its Communist neighbour.[8]

Abortion is unnatural, alien, and condemned in many parts of the world that Westerners often assume to be barbaric and uncivilized. Yet consider some recent figures from "civilized" Britain. In 2010 in the United Kingdom there were 2,290 abortions due to what is euphemistically known as "foetal medical problems," and since 2002, a staggering 26 unborn babies have been aborted because there were fears that they might suffer from a cleft palate. Of the babies killed in 2010, 482 were Down Syndrome, and a further 181 died because they had a club foot. That these figures were made public is in itself staggering, because for years now the abortion movement has used every legal and political means possible to prevent their exposure, and when we consider these numbers we can understand why. It is wrong to kill an unborn child for any reason at all, but because there is a fear that the baby – your baby – may have a cleft palate! Sometimes reason, justice, and passion simply cry out to be heard.

Even for someone who lacks any empathy for a powerless little person in the womb, surely they can see the horror of ending a life merely because once born that child may need pretty straightforward and completely safe surgery. Thing is, they almost certainly do see this. But if they allow humanity to be awarded to the unborn, they know they open the dirty doors of abortion to the light of reality: it's a human being. So while killing for a cleft palate or murdering for a club foot may seem disgraceful, the fetus is only tissue anyway, and the choice to behave selfishly is far more significant than the inherent horror of slaughtering the even mildly handicapped. So it shouldn't come as much of a surprise that babies are killed for being slightly different from the rest of the population. A cleft palate or a profound handicap present equally easy challenges in an amoral world where the self is everything. If we saw a mother beating little Johnny or Susan because they walked slowly due to a club foot, or spoke with a slight defect because of a cleft palate, we would be angry and would intervene. The police would be called, social workers would arrive, newspapers would pounce. Yet when these children are not beaten, but killed, we respond with indifference.

Postscript: Rose was a young, attractive woman and very much in love with the man she had recently married. Village life had never been easy in their part of Poland, but a combination of hard work and God's grace kept them in one piece. The crops grew, the sun shone, and she had just found out that she was pregnant. She was part of a Jewish family that had arrived almost five hundred years earlier, and had known darkness and light. But by 1890, the Russians were in control and there was much state-sanctioned anti-Semitism. Mobs of drunken men would raid, rape, and murder. It was, said the patriarch of the clan, time to move on. So with tears in their eyes for the land and for the many local people who had been their friends, they packed up what little they owned and by cart and foot moved westwards.

The journey was hard at first, but soon became agony. As borders were crossed, villages entered and passed, the group of refugees sometimes met charity, sometimes indifference, but too often downright hostility. They were stoned in one place. But on they went, knowing that there was no other direction in which to travel. Rose was showing by now, and told the assembled cousins, aunts, uncles, and community that she was expecting a baby. Her husband gripped her hand as she shared the good news. Of course they were pleased, they wanted her to know that. But she had to realize that the trip was far from over, and that it would be almost impossible for her in a few weeks. One man stepped forward to have his say. He had served in the Russian army for half his life after being kidnapped from his home when a teenager. He still had the ring that was put through his ear inscribed with the words, "Property of the Tsar." He had seen much. "They will not let you on boats and trains if they see you're with child," he said. "You'll lose the baby anyway. Better to lose it now and save yourself."

Rose felt her head swim. She had heard about these things going on, but had never heard them suggested. This man wanted her to kill her baby, to get rid of it, to have an abortion. *No,* she said. *No, no, no.* She would not do such a thing, never. And then she cried. A very old woman put her arms around Rose and whispered in Yiddish, "Don't do what they say, but do what you know to be right."

"But how do I know what is right?" Rose asked.

"Listen to your conscience, which is made and formed by God," the old woman replied.

Rose was not very religious, not compared to some, but the words left an impression. She ran to her husband, who simply held her and said only that it was their child, but that she had to carry it and that it was her life that was at risk on the journey.

Onwards they went. The snow and the cold stopped, the land became less harsh, the people more open. The baby grew bigger. Finally, after what seemed like an endless story of horror, they reached a port, larger than anything Rose had ever seen. She could barely walk now, and she had terrible pains in her stomach. She thought the baby might be dead. The former soldier had been right in most of his warnings, and in predicting that they would be denied passage on a ship because of her state. The captain of the ancient steamer they approached said he couldn't take her. She pleaded, but he understood not a word. Then she felt a cramp, so bad that she bent over. The hardened, rough old captain rushed to help her. As he did so, he looked into her eyes. A pause. "All right," he shouted, "just this once. Go on, climb aboard before I change my mind."

They boarded, and arrived safely in London, England, the next day, where they settled. And where Rose, my great-grandmother, gave birth to my grandmother, who gave birth to my father. Thank you, Grandma. For life.

———

Is abortion a choice? No, it's the taking of a pure, innocent, unborn life. Christians understand that, and it's a tragedy that they are too often dismissed and ignored.

X

WHAT ELSE CAN WE THROW AT CHRISTIANS?

WELL, QUITE A LOT CAN BE THROWN AT CHRISTIANS, really, and not all of it fits conveniently into the previous chapters. One attack we hear a great deal of the time is that Christians, particularly if they are orthodox Roman Catholic or evangelical, are right-wing, conservative, even reactionary. There is nothing at all wrong with being conservative, of course, but we need to establish why there is often, but by no means inevitably, a link between orthodox Christianity and in particular social conservatism. This is not necessarily economic conservatism, although history teaches that a free economy is far more likely to embrace religious tolerance and thus Christian freedom than a strictly socialist economy. Social conservatism, however, has become closely identified with serious Christianity, structured around Biblical beliefs and Gospel-based justice. It is considered, sophisticated, and worthy of respect. What I offer here does not intend to be in any way exclusive, but helpful and in the best sense provocative – to provoke a response from those people who would rather pigeonhole, caricature, and dismiss Christian politics.

There is no explicit and distinct credo around which Christian social conservatives gather, but there are certain principles and unchanging ideas and ideals that help to illuminate social conservatism. These consist of a belief that the family and the community, rather than the individual, is the basis of society and that without strong families and the legal and constitutional defence of same, society will disintegrate. A belief that the ideal and natural family is composed of a man and a woman and their children. A belief that single-parent families do, of course, occur and while capable of being vital and valid units, often involving heroic sacrifice, are not desirable and should not be seen in any way as ideal. A belief that same-sex couples do not constitute families in the normative sense, and that when science is exploited to give such people children it is a wrong and immoral use of science. A belief that marriage can only be between a man and a woman. A belief that life begins at conception and ends at natural death and that abortion is the taking of the life of a pre-born or un-born child. A belief that euthanasia is unacceptable, no matter how compassionate some people allegedly and wrongly think it to be. A belief that the state has not only a right, but a duty, to intervene in some areas of personal life. Censorship of pornography, for example, is a valid expression of government, as is the control of prostitution or of certain forms of hateful speech.

A belief that economic freedom, while desirable, does not necessarily guarantee a good and fair society, and is not an end in itself nor, if it is embraced in a moral vacuum, even a means to an end. A belief that any nation-state has a responsibility to guard its borders, and that while immigration is essential and valuable it may, must, also be controlled. The needs of the host population as well as the potential citizen must be taken into account, and while compassion must always be a key factor in deciding who is allowed into a country, it is vital that the needs of that nation's economy be taken into account. A state also has the responsibility to guarantee that newcomers are not criminals and are prepared to work and observe the manners of the nation. While issues of colour, race, and religion are irrelevant, issues of national commitment and respect for democracy, family, and the rule of law are vital. Countries have identities and must be more than a collection of economically profitable shopping malls. A belief that while the individual has a fundamental right to be free, he has to be free within the limits of an ethical society, and that one person's freedom must not infringe on that of others. The freedom, for example, to use illegal drugs or to promote violence is not freedom at all, but glorified selfishness. A belief that we do not live in splendid isolation but in far more splendid union with others.

A belief that while not every citizen believes in God, organized religion and the Judeo-Christian concepts that formed modern Europe and North America must be respected and honoured, and that we are all products of natural law and directly influenced by its ramifications. A belief that tradition is a binding, unifying, and positive force, and that faith, honour, duty, authority, and patriotism are constants. A belief in equality under the law, irrespective of race, gender, or religion. A belief that while human beings are capable of noble, great, and even angelic acts, their natures are not perfect and often have to be controlled by the state. A belief that a democratically elected government, supported by an independent judiciary, is the only legitimate body that can form laws and exercise state authority.

The issue of homosexuality is another subject that polarizes countries and, thus, conservatives within those countries. Some in the Christian social conservative movement have been caught up in the essentially liberal and modernistic concept of tolerance. They are convinced that a good person is a tolerant person and a very good person is an extremely tolerant person. A tolerance of differing opinions or of a different religion is, of course, absolutely essential and an indication of civilization. Indeed, Christian social conservatism regards such tolerance as an essential foundation. But the modern world has reinterpreted tolerance to mean something entirely different – the refusal to pass an opinion and to discern the difference between right and wrong, to indulge in moral equivalents. Ironically, when Christian social conservatives do express their opinions about what is right and wrong they are attacked and abused by "tolerant" liberals as being "intolerant."

For some neo-conservatives, for example, the argument over homosexuality goes further. As they believe that every person is primarily an economic unit, their sexual activity is really quite irrelevant. Many Christian social conservatives, on the other hand, believe that we are creatures, made with a specific purpose and intended to follow a specific way of life. Homosexuality, while to be tolerated in an open and free society, is not to be encouraged or treated on an equal footing with heterosexuality. Man and woman are more, much more, than the sum of their economic worth. Procreation is not the sole purpose of marriage, but it is a crucial one. If homosexuals can be married to each other, why not brothers and sisters? What about polygamy? If love is the only criterion for a valid marriage, we are being philosophically arbitrary if we claim that a man can love a man and a woman a woman, but a brother not love a sister, and a man not love five wives. It is also naive and disingenuous to argue that if homosexual couples are acknowledged by the state, and by some liberal Christian churches, as being married, it does not alter life for the majority of people. Such an act directly dents the importance and validity of authentic, heterosexual marriage. The actions of the individual affect more than the individual who takes the action and the individuals around them. These actions also affect the entire community.

Then we have the issues of pornography and censorship. Many conservatives are reluctant to indulge in censorship, believing that in a perfect world the individual should be allowed complete freedom of expression and freedom to read. This was a tenable position at one time, but no longer. As Christian social conservatives themselves are repeatedly told, times do change. A 1914 pacifism in the face of the Kaiser's foolishness, for example, would be completely different from a 1939 pacifism in the face of the Fuhrer's Nazism. While opponents of censorship delight in mocking the rather absurd banning of books such as *Lady Chatterley's Lover* or even the delightful Tintin cartoons, they fail or refuse to look at the current situation.

Take, for example, the case of Dennis Cooper, a writer highly regarded in some circles. He is championed by many as just the sort of author the state has no right to regulate. Let us take one of his stories, a work entitled *Frisk*. Here a fifteen-year-old boy is murdered for sexual kicks, he is humiliated and hit, he is tortured, and his rectum is used for gruesome and grotesque purposes. "He opened his eyes very wide," writes Cooper. "Otherwise he didn't fight me at all. It takes a lot longer to strangle someone than you'd think." The victim is fifteen. Or, from the same piece, an account of the rape, sexual beating, and murder of a boy whose excrement the narrator has just eaten. The victim's penis is cut in two and he is decapitated. The narrator masturbates over this. Friends arrive. "They kicked the corpse around for a while. This created a pretty hilarious fireworks display of blood." Or how about a repugnantly graphic story by one Ann Wertheim about incestuous rape. In this elaborately constructed lesbian fantasy, the victim is shown as enjoying herself as she welcomes agonizing penetration, oral sex, and physical violence from her father.[1]

Both of these stories appeared in a book titled *Forbidden Passages*, a collection of banned writings that, paradoxically, is now available in North America and most of Europe. Of the last piece, one of the compilers of the anthology wrote that when it came into her office "several of us nearly fainted from intense levels of sexual heat." Now imagine if we read of a group of Klansmen describing the beating, torture, and murder of a black teenager, with graphic detail and description, and then read in an introduction to a collection of banned writings that one of the editorial staff almost fainted over this particular story because of the racist passion in the office. Both involve an innocent, bewildered victim, both involve breaking both the moral and the civil law, and both would be anathema to societal standards. The Christian social conservative response would be to intervene in such a case. With hate literature, Holocaust denial, and the like, we can at least defeat these rancid ideas with simple fact. But the literary depiction of sadistic pedophilia and the sexual torture of children is not about fact but about a basic immoral stance.

The questions often asked are, where do we draw the line and who is to do the drawing? The answers are not as complex as some would have us believe, and need not be extreme or even noticeable to the overwhelming majority of people. We draw lines of limitation every day and give politicians, judges, police officers, and teachers the authority to use ethical pencils. Individual customs officers, overworked and unqualified, are not the most suitable guardians of our literary borders, but there is no reason why a panel of judges should not decide on what is allowed to enter the country. We allow, after all, such a system to control the flow of people, and it is surely axiomatic that one book is capable of much more harm than a single man or woman. Christian conservatism is a living ideology, and as such it has to be able to adapt and to change, without losing sight of its essentials.

It is also about practicality and about practical politics. Its oxygen is reality. It was and is produced by the world and the world's events; it is unlike other political beliefs, conceived only to shape the world and the world's events. Take the case of women wanting to appear topless in public. This is permitted in some parts of Europe and North America, but not in others. To Christian social conservatives, this is a case of social engineering, the forced and contrived elimination of gender differences, an aggressive change to existing societal standards, and a fundamental attack upon society and community. The arguments put forward by the equality fanatics are that because men are permitted to bare their chests, women should be allowed the same right. Women's breasts, however, are directly sexual, the second most erogenous part of a woman's body, and are also more biologically intimate in that they are used for nursing children. Also, only certain types of men would walk along the streets topless, because a thin T-shirt prevents sunburn and may deflect heat. Be they the owners of beer-bellies or perfect pectorals, those men who want to show their upper bodies to the greater world are usually making a deeper, more neurotic point. We should be dissuading them, not persuading others. The only generally acceptable form of exposure is during nursing, when we should encourage women to feed their children whenever and wherever they want. Breast-feeding represents much of what is best about humanity, such as love, procreation, and family. But the public exposure represents the precise opposite of the nursing scenario, and their behaviour is the contrary of natural. It is full, not of care and bonding, but of egotism and perversity. A very different response to the usual caricature of what Christians think of this issue, in which they are painted as being either aroused, intimidated, or simply stupid.

Another issue involving personal behaviour is prostitution. The Christian social conservative argument is that prostitution involves several people. The man paying the money, the woman giving herself, the pimp, and the rest of us who make up general society. The man with the cash may, if prostitution is illegal and not accepted, merely have his freedom restricted, but not so the prostitute. There are very few women who willingly prostitute themselves, but many who do so out of economic desperation. A single mother in near poverty is not acting from her own free will. As for the wider community, I have yet to hear any convincing argument that our physical, spiritual, ethical, or educational well-being is in any way improved by allowing prostitution. I have, however, heard many arguments that permitting such an indulgence eats away at the very core of our society. There is such a thing as collective responsibility.

Then come the arguments concerning the free market. For a market to be genuinely free, the participants must enjoy something like equal rights and privileges. A union stranglehold or a business monopoly prevents true economic liberty. So what of the pimps and pushers? Those who are so concerned with the free market would do well to read the arguments of those men in the last century who employed ten-year-old chimney sweeps. They said the boys were not being forced into the work and that the lads were paid and cared for. Because the society of the time had less refined and sensitive views toward child labour, it accepted such a defence. Yet when reformers educated that society, the arguments of the child exploiters suddenly blew away like dirty ashes. The same will happen if, and when, we educate our society about the reality of unfettered commercialism and its ethical consequences. The state has a right to limit and control the outer limits of the market so such a market can be, in the most authentic sense, truly free.

Last comes the issue of morality. We impose something like a universal morality a great deal of the time, precisely because it is considered universal. Those who argue that the state has no right to decide what is right and wrong put themselves in a contradictory position. They come to their conclusions in the first place solely because they themselves have their own theories of right and wrong and, consequently, impose them on the state and its decisions.

Much of all this concerns how we perceive the nature of state, government, and authority. A healthy fear and mistrust of the state is surely a good thing. But we also have to understand the difference between gratuitous state intervention and essential government regulation. Christian social conservatism accepts the place of the state and sees it not always as a last resort, but often as a constructive regulator and intervener. Consider a group of people playing a team sport. They are given complete freedom, in that there is no referee, no uniforms, and no rules. They foul each other, hurt each other, have no idea what is going on, and end up fighting. They are truly free, but are not truly happy. What should have been a magnificent sport became an ugly mess. Then consider the team sport in which there are too many rules and the referee is officious and intrusive. The sport becomes a slow, muddy annoyance. The participants are neither free nor happy.

There is, however, a middle way. The rules can be applied intelligently and fairly. The referee can be accountable and understanding, while the players are responsible and, knowing that the referee understands the game, observe the rules. The result is the game as it should be played, with the maximum enjoyment for the maximum number of players. The truly offensive and violent players are taken off. The participants are free in the real sense and happy in a meaningful sense.

The modern state is feared and despised for good reason. It indulges in ludicrous interventions into our daily lives and often seems intent on extending its own power simply for the sake of power itself. But a greater accountability, a change in the electoral process, and a more actively political population could change this, without requiring the disappearance of the state itself. For example, there are currently attempts being made in North America to make it a crime for parents to spank their children. An absurd and offensive example of state interference, often initiated by people who do not have any children. But the state already makes it illegal for parents to physically assault their children, which is surely a good thing. It is the nature of the state and the extent of its power, not its very existence, which has to be questioned.

That great Christian social conservative, the British journalist and broadcaster Malcolm Muggeridge, once said that "without moral order, a society can have no real order at any level."[2] Now this is interesting. Because many of those who preach freedom seem to be unaware of this surely self-evident fact. The liberty of the swimmer to float out to sea is actually better known as drowning. There is no example in history of authentic progress without authentic order. Nations and empires were only economically and culturally productive when they were relatively ordered societies, with a suitably strong government. Further, when the moral order of those societies began to decay, economic and political collapse quickly followed. The Roman Empire is only one example of this. First came moral disintegration, then political catastrophe, then what we now think of as the Dark Ages. Many Christian social conservatives believe that a new dark age may be upon us unless we rethink our ways. The state is being used to end human life rather than to save it. It is being used to open our borders to damaging and obscene literature rather than guarding them against such material. Do we have a prayer?

Of course we do, and prayer is at the very centre of Christianity, and something else Christians are mocked for believing. "When we pray to God we must be seeking nothing – nothing," said Saint Francis of Assisi. P.J. Wingate believed that "'Give us this day our daily bread' is probably the most perfectly constructed and useful sentence ever set down in the English language." And Søren Kierkegaard wrote, "I have been driven many times to my knees by the overwhelming conviction that I had nowhere else to go." Abraham Lincoln: "Prayer does not change God, but it changes him who prays." U.S. president Woodrow Wilson was practical as well as spiritual with "Business underlies everything in our national life, including our spiritual life. Witness the fact that in the Lord's Prayer, the first petition is for daily bread. No one can worship God or love his neighbor on an empty stomach." Whether prayer is efficacious or not depends on what we believe prayer to be. For the Christian, it is the open communication between the person at prayer and that person's Maker. God always hears prayers and always answers them, although sometimes the answer is no. The difference between a loving God refusing us and a God not hearing us is about as basic and easy to understand as we can get, but we live in an age when being refused is even worse than being ignored. "I think the reason we sometimes have the false sense that God is so far away is because that is where we have put him," says the Christian author and apologist Ravi Zacharias. "We have kept him at a distance, and then when we are in need and call on him in prayer, we wonder where he is. He is exactly where we left him."

My sister Stephanie is six years older than me and lives in Britain. We never really got on. I wish it was otherwise, but there we are. We simply never got on. We argued. A lot. Steph also argued with my parents. A lot. Steph married and had a daughter, Tessa, but her marriage broke down after a few years and the family tensions grew even worse. After the collapse, she had some dreadful rows with me and with our parents, until after one particularly venomous episode she cut off all contact. Neither she nor her daughter, whom my parents had partly raised, would speak to any of us again. This was all some years ago, and in the meantime I married a Canadian and left Britain to live in Toronto. So it wasn't so bad for me, three thousand miles away from the mess. But it was hell for my parents. Steph got married again and had a second child. Now there were two grandchildren living in Britain and my parents could see neither of them. One of them they had never seen at all.

As the years went by, the tears dried up and a dark resignation replaced the feverish anguish that had been so difficult to tolerate. A scab formed over the wound. I had tried to make contact with Steph, but I didn't even know her new married name. Hard to trace someone without their name. We didn't even know in which town she lived. I pray. I have to, it's what Christians do. I had, though, never prayed for a family reunion, probably because I was afraid of the "no" answer. Then one day, and for some reason I do not know, I asked God for the family to be reunited. Just a brief prayer, but heartfelt and sincere. A week later the telephone rang. It was my mum, in her wonderful cockney accent that still made me feel warm and safe. "Mike," she said. "You're not going to believe this. I've got a letter here from Stephanie." A long pause. "She says she wants to make up, to meet." I listened, hardly registering what was being said. "I don't know what to do," she continued. "I'm frightened of starting all the pain again."

My sister had not spoken to my parents in fifteen years. Suddenly I prayed for a resolution. My mother received a letter from my sister four days later, meaning that she almost certainly wrote it the same day that I asked for help. This was strange, this was frightening, this was remarkable. There was a phone number on the letter. I called it. A man answered. "Is Steph there?" I asked. He wanted to know who it was. I told him. I then heard him tell Stephanie and I heard her saying my name over and over again, as though if she stopped I would no longer be there. She was crying, almost hysterically. She came to the phone and in between gulps for air she asked me why I hadn't made contact earlier. I told her I didn't know how to. Why, I responded, hadn't she contacted me? Because, she explained, she kept hearing that we all hated her. When I asked her who had said this, she couldn't remember, almost as though the thought was implanted.

I then asked why she had decided to break the silence. "Because I heard that Dad was very ill and I just couldn't have lived with myself if I hadn't spoken to him." At this point I choked a little. "But Steph, he's fine. He's not ill at all." We chatted, we laughed, we cried. Then I said to her that I had to reveal something that was very important, something that had changed my life forever. I told her that on a specific date some years ago I had become a Christian. She didn't answer at first. Then she asked me to repeat the date. I felt a warmth, a sensation that was real yet beyond detailed description. "Mike," she said, her voice shaking, "so did I. Oh my God, so did I."

Let's end with our end. Death, and what surrounds it. Rather like the abortion debate, Christians are condemned because of their involvement in the campaign against euthanasia or, to use any of its other current descriptions, mercy killing, compassionate homicide, or assisted suicide. Pride hides beneath most that is wrong, from the thinnest of failings to the fattest of crime. The pride that leads us to believe that we, rather than God, are always in control and that our bodies are ours to do with what we want, whenever we want. Sometimes this attitude is invincibly malicious, sometimes almost understandable. When it comes to the subject of euthanasia, we see both aspects. For those promoting what amounts to a cult of death, it is horror, pure and simple. For those who are suffering, the subject is far more complex and delicate. The arguments *for* euthanasia are perhaps better known than those against it, because we hear them publicly articulated on a fairly regular basis. Implicit, but perhaps not consciously so, in this approach is the notion that disability is a curse, that we have the right and wisdom to make our own decisions about when to die, and that so-called mercy killing is administered only after layers of consideration. If at all possible, nobody approaching death should experience pain, and experts in the field now know that nobody need do so. All physical pain can be controlled, but insufficient time and money is spent training doctors and nurses how to deal with end-of-life challenges.

The proposition that a person who feels that they want to die is making an objective, informed decision about whether to live or die is fatuous. In reality, they are the least qualified people because they are, yes, so terrified and agonized that they want to die. Any of us who has experienced any sort of pain or nausea know that it is difficult to see beyond the immediate need to be free of distress. Beyond the physical pressures are the emotional ones. The feeling that one doesn't fit in any longer, the attitude that "I've had a good life, the children could do so much with the inheritance I'll leave behind, it costs them so much money to keep me in the home and I know the grandchildren don't like coming all this way to visit me all the time." The media tells them that only the young and sexy matter; they are made to feel by television and radio that life is over by the age of seventeen, there are anti-aging stores opening on the high street, and then we wonder why elderly people feel rejected. A culture that once revered the aged as temples of wisdom now looks on them as slums of irrelevance. The answer is not to help someone die, but help them to live.

It is no accident that the people most intimidated by, and active against, euthanasia are the disabled. While we boast equality, we violently discriminate against disability at the earliest opportunity by aborting babies that are considered imperfect, and then attempt to pass legislation and create a cultural shift that would make the life of disabled people easier to terminate in their more mature years. In 1993 in Canada, for example, a man called Robert Latimer killed his little girl Tracy. She had cerebral palsy but did not ask to die, was surrounded by people who loved her, and even by extraordinary people who were willing to adopt her if her care became too difficult for the Latimers. Mr. Latimer put her in the family car, poisoned her to death with carbon monoxide, and then put her body into his wife's bed, hoping the girl's mother and the authorities would believe that Tracy had died naturally. His crime was discovered and his defence was that he was putting her out of her misery, when, of course, he was putting her out of his. When Latimer was arrested and charged, and especially after he was imprisoned, media campaigns and petitions sprang up to support him. Almost all the time the defence was at work, it hardly ever mentioned the rights of the little girl who had been murdered. It took a child writing in the *Vancouver Sun* newspaper in 1994 to show another side of the issue.

My name is Teague. I am 11 years old and have really severe cerebral palsy. The Latimer case in Saskatchewan has caused me a great deal of unhappiness and worry over the past few weeks. I feel very strongly that all children are valuable and deserve to live full and complete lives. No one should make the decision of another person about whether their life is worth living or not.

I have a friend who had CP and he decided that life was too hard and too painful. So he really let himself die. I knew he was leaving this world and letting himself dwell in the spiritual world. I told him that I understood that the spiritual world was really compelling, but that life was worth fighting for. I had to fight to live when I was very sick. The doctors said I wouldn't live long, but I knew I had so much to accomplish still.

I have to fight pain all the time. When I was little life was pain, I couldn't remember no pain. My foster Mom Cara helped me learn to manage and control my pain. Now my life is so full of joy. There isn't time enough in the day for me to learn and experience all I wish to. I have a family and many friends who love me. I have a world of knowledge to discover. I have so much to give.

I can't walk or talk or feed myself. But I am not "suffering from cerebral palsy." I use a wheelchair, but I am not "confined to a wheelchair." I have pain, but I do not need to be "put out of my misery."

My body is not my enemy. It is that which allows me to enjoy Mozart, experience Shakespeare, savour a bouillabaisse feast and cuddle my Mom. Life is a precious gift. It belongs to the person to whom it was given. Not to her parents, nor to the state. Tracy's life was hers "to make of it what she could." My life is going to be astounding.

We have to be extremely careful when we use terms like "quality of life," because they are entirely subjective and, anyway, largely without meaning. I see people who are physically and mentally able all the time who have no obvious quality of life. They seem to do no good to or for others, they are selfish, lazy, foolish, rude, arrogant. Such a life does not seem to be one of any genuine quality. Equally there are millions of people, often living in slum conditions and working in mundane, empty jobs, whose quality of life may be questioned. Or wealthy, privileged, but spiritually bankrupt, vacuous men and women who contribute little but take so much. They appear to have no quality of life, and thus have no need to be alive. It depends who has the power and who is able to make the decisions. In the 1890s and early twentieth century, social engineers and eugenicists advocated an entire systematic program to eliminate those whom they considered to be lacking in quality of life.

Beyond the intellectually flimsy and morally dangerous definition of "quality of life," there are also semantic difficulties with words such as "terminal." One of the champions of euthanasia, Dr. Jack Kevorkian, when speaking to the National Press Club in Washington, D.C., in 1992, said that a terminal illness was "any disease that curtails life even for a day," and the Hemlock Society, one of the largest and most active pro-euthanasia organizations in the world, frequently uses the word "terminal" as part of the phrase "terminal old age," which has sweeping implications. Doctors generally admit that estimates of life expectancy are extremely difficult and dangerous to make, and while informed estimates of life expectancy certainly have a place in medicine, there are numerous people every year who live far longer, even years longer, than expected. Sometimes this means a great deal more money is required to keep them alive and keep them well, and that means more personal investment from families, and more public investment from governments providing institutionalized health care, and from insurance companies providing private insurance. The idea that financial concerns are not taken into account in the realm of euthanasia is naive in the extreme. Then, of course, we have the slippery slope argument, often dismissed by supporters of euthanasia as being hysterical. Yet some slopes are slippery, very slippery indeed.

Margaret Somerville is a bioethicist of international reputation. In 2010, she wrote,

Although the need for euthanasia to relieve pain and suffering is the justification given, and the one the public accepts in supporting its legalization, research shows that dying people request euthanasia far more frequently because of fear of social isolation and of being a burden on others, than pain. So, should avoiding loneliness or being a burden count as a sufficient justification? Recently, some pro-euthanasia advocates have gone further, arguing that respect for people's rights to autonomy and self-determination means competent adults have a right to die at a time of their choosing, and the state has no right to prevent them from doing so. In other words, if euthanasia were legalized, the state has no right to require a justification for its use by competent, freely consenting adults.

She concluded,

Initially, euthanasia was limited to terminally ill, competent adults, with unrelievable pain and suffering, who repeatedly asked for euthanasia and gave their informed consent to it. Now, none of those requirements necessarily applies, in some cases not even in theory and, in others, not in practice.[3]

Life is not a sentence, but a blessing. Death is guaranteed, but to encourage it is a curse, especially for those who are most vulnerable and do not have access to power, money, friends, and even the basic tools of appeal. These are the most likely victims of euthanasia, those who are so ill as to have lost the ability to speak, write, and communicate. To abandon these people would be horrible, uncaring, and, in a very real sense, utterly heretical.

Which brings us to the conclusion of the book. Christians are not demanding centre stage in the public square, or to be at the heart of the body politic. But they are asking to be allowed into that square, and permitted a place somewhere on the body. Followers of Christ are silenced by deliberate exclusion, and also forced into virtual invisibility by lies and distortion. Criticize Christianity for what it says and does, but not for what it does not say or do. Give it and its adherents the basic courtesy of understanding its history and beliefs, before condemning it. Give it, simply, the same respect you would any other ideology or theology. Christians ask, not for privileges, but for permission – to be heard properly, understood authentically, embraced or rejected seriously. Heresy originally meant choice; there is no choice without knowledge, and no knowledge without truth. Be a heretic if you like, but be one worth the name.

ACKNOWLEDGEMENTS

NUMEROUS PEOPLE HAVE HELPED ME WRITE THIS BOOK — some of them by their learning and their ability to teach what is true and good, and others by their lack of learning and their ability, sometimes unwittingly, to teach the nature of error and untruth. To both groups of people I owe a great debt of gratitude. The latter shall remain nameless because it would be unfair to embarrass them and, anyway, they tend to receive far too much attention already. To the former, that you know who you are is sufficient praise. To my publisher at McClelland & Stewart, Doug Pepper, and to my editor, Jenny Bradshaw, I owe more than I can say.

NOTES

CHAPTER ONE

JESUS DIDN'T EXIST AND CHRISTIANITY IS A
LATER CREATION

1. Ferguson, Everett, *Backgrounds of Early Christianity*,
   Eerdmans, 1993.
2. *Ibid.*
3. Scott, J. Julius, Jr., *Jewish Backgrounds of the New Testament*,
   Baker, 2000.
4. *Ibid.*
5. Mounder, Chris, *Documents of the Christian Church*, Oxford,
   1999.
6. *Ibid.*
7. *Ibid.*
8. *Ibid.*
9. *Ibid.*
10. *Ibid.*
11. *Ibid.*

CHAPTER TWO

THERE IS NO GOD, BAD THINGS HAPPEN TO
GOOD PEOPLE, AND SO ON

1. Hooper, Walter, *C.S. Lewis: A Companion and Guide*,
   HarperCollins, 1996.
2. Collins, Francis, *The Language of God: A Scientist Presents
   Evidence for Belief*, Simon & Schuster, 1997.
3. Dawkins, Richard, *The God Delusion*, Bantam, 2006.

4. Chesterton, G.K., *Heretics*, Hendrickson, 2009.

5. *The Philosophical Writings of Descartes*, Cambridge, 1985.

CHAPTER THREE

THE DA VINCI CODE

1. Strobel, Lee, and Gary Poole, *Exploring* The Da Vinci Code, Zondervan, 2006.

2. *Ibid.*

3. Ferguson, Everett, *Backgrounds of Early Christianity*, Eerdmans, 1993.

4. *Ibid.*

5. Stephenson, Paul, *Constantine*, Overlook, 2010.

6. *Ibid.*

7. Allen, John, *Opus Dei*, Doubleday, 2005.

CHAPTER FOUR

ALL THE CLEVER PEOPLE ARE ATHEISTS.
OR, CHRISTIANS ARE STUPID

1. Hooper, Walter, *C.S. Lewis: A Companion and Guide*, HarperCollins, 1996.

2. *The Lion, the Witch and the Wardrobe*, HarperCollins, 2002.

3. Hooper, Walter, *C.S. Lewis: A Companion and Guide*, HarperCollins, 1996.

4. Carpenter, Humphrey, *J.R.R. Tolkien*, Allen & Unwin, 1988.

5. *The Letters of J.R.R. Tolkien*, Houghton Mifflin, 1981.

6. Reynolds, Barbara, *Dorothy L. Sayers*, Hodder & Stoughton, 1993.

7. Ingrams, Richard, *Muggeridge*, HarperCollins, 1995.

8. Wilson, A.N., *Hilaire Belloc*, Atheneum, 1984.

9. Ker, Ian, *G.K. Chesterton*, Oxford, 2010.

10. Hastings, Selina, *Evelyn Waugh*, Houghton Mifflin, 1994.

CHAPTER FIVE
HITLER WAS A CHRISTIAN

1. *Hitler's Table Talk 1941–1944*, Oxford University Press.
2. *Ibid.*
3. *Ibid.*
4. Speech to Reichstag, January, 1939.
5. Gilbert, Sir Martin, *The Righteous*, Key Porter, 2003.
6. Dalin, Rabbi David G., *The Myth of Hitler's Pope*, Regnery, 2005.
7. *Ibid.*
8. *Ibid.*
9. *Ibid.*
10. Gilbert, Sir Martin, *The Righteous*, Key Porter, 2003.
11. Lapide, Pinchas, *Three Popes and the Jews*, Souvenir Press, 1967.

CHAPTER SIX
CHRISTIANS AND CHRISTIANITY SUPPORTED SLAVERY

1. Belmonte, Kevin, *William Wilberforce*, Zondervan, 2002.
2. *Ibid.*
3. *Ibid.*
4. *Proceedings of Ohio State Christian Anti-Slavery Convention 1859*, Nabu, 2010.
5. *Ibid.*

CHAPTER SEVEN
CHRISTIANS ARE OPPOSED TO SCIENCE

1. *The Opus Majus of Roger Bacon*, Cambridge, 2010.
2. *Ibid.*
3. Fara, Patrick, *Science: A Four Thousand Year History*, Oxford, 2010.
4. *Ibid.*
5. Heilbron, John, *Galileo*, Oxford, 2010.

CHAPTER EIGHT
CHRISTIANS OPPOSE PROGRESS AND CHANGE

1. Hammond, J.L., *Lord Shaftesbury*, Kessinger, 2007.
2. Livingstone, David, *Missionary Travels and Researches in South Africa*, Leffmann, 2010.
3. Hatton, Jean, *Betsy: The Dramatic Biography of Prison Reformer Elizabeth Fry*, Kregel, 2006.
4. Bostridge, Mark, *Florence Nightingale: The Making of an Icon*, Farrar, Straus and Giroux, 2008.
5. Collins, Kenneth J, *The Theology of John Wesley: Holy Love and the Shape of Grace*, Abingdon, 2007.

CHAPTER NINE
CHRISTIANS ARE OBSESSED WITH ABORTION

1. Clowes, Dr. Brian, *The Facts of Life,* HLI, 1997.
2. George, Robert P., and Christopher Tollefsen, *Embryo: A Defence of Human Life,* Doubleday, 2008.
3. Klusendorf, Scott, *The Case for Life,* Crossway, 2009.
4. *Ibid.*
5. *Ibid.*
6. U.N. Population Database, 2008.
7. Food and Agriculture Organisation, UN, 2007.
8. Kasun, Jacqueline, *War Against Population*, Ignatius, 1988.

CHAPTER TEN
WHAT ELSE CAN WE THROW AT CHRISTIANS?

1. Califia, Pat, *Forbidden Passages*, Cleis, 1995.
2 Ingrams, Richard, *Muggeridge*, HarperCollins, 1995.
3. Clowes, Dr. Brian, *The Facts of Life,* HLI, 1997.

BIBLIOGRAPHY

THERE ARE LIBRARIES OF BOOKS covering the subjects discussed in this slim volume, and this bibliography is merely an introduction to the range of further reading. Each of the books recommended here will contain its own bibliography and references.

Beckwith, Francis, and Gregory Koukl, *Relativism* (Beckwith, Baker, 1998)

Beckwith, Francis, William Craig, and J.P. Lindsley, *Art, True Truth: Defending Absolute Truth in a Relativistic World* (IVP, 2004)

Blanchard, John, *Has Science Got Rid of God?* (Evangelical Press, 2004)

Blankenhorn, David, *The Future of Marriage* (Encounter, 2007)

Bock, Darrell, and Daniel Wallace, *Dethroning Jesus: Exposing Popular Culture's Quest to Unseat the Biblical Christ* (Thomas Nelson, 2007)

Burleigh, Michael, *Earthly Powers* (Harper Collins, 2005)

Burleigh, Michael, *Sacred Causes* (Harper Collins, 2007)

Carroll, Warren, *A History of Christendom*, 5 vols (Christendom Press, 1987–2010)

Carson, D.A., *The Gagging of God: Christianity Confronts Pluralism* (Zondervan, 1996)

Chesterton, G.K., *Heretics* (London, 1905)

Chesterton, G.K., *The Everlasting Man* (Ignatius, 1993)

Clowes, Dr. Brian, *The Facts of Life* (HLI, 1997)

Coffin, Patrick, *Sex Au Naturel* (Emmaus Road, 2010)

Collins, Roger, *Keepers of the Keys of Heaven* (Basic, 2009)

Copan, Paul, *Loving Wisdom: Christian Philosophy of Religion* (Chalice Press, 2007)

Crean, Thomas, *A Catholic Replies to Professor Dawkins* (Family Publications, 2007)

D'Souza, Dinesh, *What's So Great About Christianity* (Regnery, 2007)

Dalin, Rabbi David G., *The Myth of Hitler's Pope* (Regnery, 2005)

Daniel-Rops, H., *The Church in an Age of Revolution* (Dent, 1965)

Duffy, Eamon, *The Stripping of the Altars* (Yale, 2005)

Evans, Craig, *Fabricating Jesus: How Modern Scholars Distort the Gospels* (IVP, 2006)

Flew, Antony, *There Is a God: How the World's Most Notorious Atheist Changed His Mind* (HarperOne, 2007)

Garrison, Becky, *The New Atheist Crusaders* (Thomas Nelson, 2007)

Geisler, Norman, and Frank Turek, *I Don't Have Enough Faith to Be an Atheist* (Crossway Books, 2004)

Geisler, Norman, and Ron Brooks, *When Skeptics Ask* (Baker, 1990)

Geivett, Douglas, and Gary Habermas, eds., *In Defense of Miracles* (IVP, 1997)

George, Robert P., and Christopher Tollefsen, *Embryo: A Defence of Human Life* (Doubleday, 2008)

Guinness, Os, *Unspeakable: Facing up to Evil in an Age of Genocide and Terror* (Harper, 2005)

Hill, Jonathan, *What Has Christianity Ever Done for Us?* (IVP, 2005)

Hutchinson, Robert, *The Politically Incorrect Guide to the Bible* (Regnery, 2007)

Johnson, Phillip, *Darwin on Trial* (Regnery Gateway, 1991)

Jones, Dr. E. Michael, *Degenerate Moderns* (Ignatius, 1993)

Kahlenborn, Dr. Chris, *Breast Cancer* (OMS, 2000)

Kennedy, D. James, *What if Jesus Had Never Been Born?* (Thomas Nelson, 1994)

Klusendorf, Scott, *The Case for Life* (Crossway, 2009)

Komoszewski, J. Ed, James Sawyer, and Daniel Wallace, *Reinventing Jesus* (Kregel, 2006)

Kreeft, Peter, and Ronald Tacelli, *Handbook of Christian Apologetics* (IVP, 1994)

Kreeft, Peter, *A Refutation of Moral Relativism* (Ignatius, 1999)

Kreeft, Peter, *The Snakebite Letters* (Ignatius, 1991)

Kurzman, Dan, *A Special Mission* (Da Capo, 2007)

Lennox, John, *God's Undertaker: Has Science Buried God?* (Lion, 2007)

Lewis, C.S., *Miracles* (Macmillan, 1947)

Lewis, C.S., *The Problem of Pain* (Fontana, 1940)

Marshall, David, *The Truth Behind the New Atheism* (Harvest House, 2007)

McDowell, Josh, and Bob Hostetler, *The New Tolerance* (Tyndale, 1998)

McGrath, Alister, *Dawkin's God: Genes, Memes, and the Meaning of Life* (Blackwell, 2004)

McGrath, Alister, *The Dawkins' Delusion* (Intervarsity Press, 2007)

Moreland, J.P., *Christianity and the Nature of Science* (Baker, 1989)

Moreland, J.P. *To Everyone an Answer: A Case for the Christian Worldview* (IVP, 2004)

Moreland, J.P., and William Craig, *Philosophical Foundations for a Christian Worldview* (IVP, 2003)

Muggeridge, Malcolm, *Something Beautiful for God* (Collins, 1997)

Nathanson, Bernard N., *Abortion Papers: Inside the Abortion Mentality* (Frederick Fell, 1983)

Nathanson, Bernard N., *The Hand of God: A Journey from Death to Life by the Abortion Doctor Who Changed His Mind* (Regnery, 2001)

Pearcey, Nancy, *Total Truth: Liberating Christianity from its Cultural Captivity* (Crossway Books, 2004)

Reisman, Judith A., *Kinsey: Crimes and Consequences* (The Institute for Media Education, 2000)

Rhodes, Ron, *Answering the Objections of Atheists, Agnostics, and Skeptics* (Harvest House, 2006)

Roberts, Mark, *Can We Trust the Gospels?* (Crossway Books, 2007)

Schaeffer, Francis, *The God Who Is There* (IVP, 1968)

Schmidt, Alvin, *Under the Influence* (Zondervan, 2001) [reissued as *How Christianity Changed the World* (Zondervan, 2004)]

Sommer, Carl J., *We Look for a Kingdom* (Ignatius 2007)

Stark, Rodney, *For the Glory of God* (Princeton University Press, 2003)

Strobel, Lee, *The Case for a Creator* (Zondervan, 2004)

Strobel, Lee, *The Case for Christ* (Zondervan, 1998)

Strobel, Lee, *The Case for Faith* (Zondervan, 2000)

Strobel, Lee, *The Case for the Real Jesus* (Zondervan, 2007)

Waugh, Evelyn, *Edmund Campion* (Ignatius, 2005)

Weigel, George, *Witness to Hope* (Collins, 1999)

Witherington, Ben, *What Have They Done with Jesus?* (HarperSanFrancisco, 2006)

Woods, Thomas E., *How the Catholic Church Built Western Civilization* (Regnery, 2005)

Wright, N.T., *Evil and the Justice of God* (SPCK, 2006)

Zacharias, Ravi, and Norman Geisler, eds., *Who Made God?: And Answers to Over 100 Other Tough Questions of Faith* (Zondervan, 2003)

Zolli, Eugenio, *Before the Dawn* (Sheed & Ward, 1954)

MICHAEL COREN is the bestselling author of fifteen books, including biographies of G.K. Chesterton, H.G. Wells, Arthur Conan Doyle, J.R.R. Tolkien, and C.S. Lewis. He is the host of the talk show "The Arena" on the SUN News Network and also writes a syndicated column for ten daily newspapers. His most recent book, *Why Catholics Are Right*, was a national bestseller.

Please visit **michaelcoren.com**.